MW01274896

Attachment is Action: Relationship Matters

Susan's Reflections, Rants and Ruminations

A handbook for responsible adults

Susan Dafoe-Abbey, BIS, MEd

Registered Marriage and Family Therapist

Professional Associate Neufeld Institute

Cover design by Amber E. Paxton, BAA CreativeType www.creativetypecanada.com

Acknowledgements

There are two men in my life who made this book possible. One, is Dr. Gordon Neufeld, whose generosity created a role of 'Professional Associate of the Neufeld Institute' for me, so that we could preserve our relationship without my continuation as a member of his Faculty on the Neufeld Virtual Campus. Almost seven years after our first meeting in 2007 and an endless number of hours learning, teaching, practicing and consulting, I am honoured to share my use of his attachment-based, developmental paradigm through an accumulation of my reflections, rants and ruminations. I thank you Gordon, for your brilliance in "connecting the dots" and I feel privileged to have been given your blessing to pass it on to the parents, teachers and caregivers who invite me to walk the maze with them.

The other is my husband David, who has encouraged me to write, who has edited my words so that they make sense and who has committed himself to be "the" person in my life into whom I can lean. Thank you for supporting my work with your good mind, big heart and patient editorial skill.

This handbook is dedicated to my family: my father's courage, my mother's determination, my children's resilience and my grandchildren's emergence. Somehow, who we are both together and separately, becomes clearer when there is a keyboard under my fingertips. I am humbled by the power of attachment in action.

Table of Contents

Acknowledgments

Adolescents

"...constructs of co-dependence and enabling suggest there are right things to do and wrong things to do with our teenagers."

Adolescents and Giving Advice

I am very cautious about giving advice. To give advice suggests that there is a right thing to do and a right way of doing it, and if the advice were followed, success would come. For example constructs of co-dependence and enabling suggest there are right things to do and wrong things to do with our teenagers. These constructs cannot be instructed. In other words, what the parent needs to find is what is true for them with regards to their child, not what would be the right thing to do. Unless parents dig down deep to find their own truth, they will never find the strength to live it out- no matter what that direction may be. My hope is always that the parent wants to hold on.

It seems to me that if possible and if we can find the strength within us, we should try to hold on to the ones we love, through thick and thin. But we cannot make anyone else do this, and if they try to hold on because of some advice they have received from me, they won't be able to dig deep enough to find the strength to carry them through. Many of their friends and relatives will advise them to back off, because they can't stand the suffering that comes from experiencing failure after failure. It is natural to want to rescue the ones we care about from this fate. Nor should we stand in judgment of someone who has come to the end of their rope. We must all find our own truth and then dig down deep to live it out.

For those that want to hold on, we should let them know, that love is never futile. If it doesn't change the person we love, it will most certainly change us. I have seen parents absolutely transformed by their futile attempts to save a loved one, if they are capable of enduring the grief that results, that is. Their efforts may not be enough to save the adolescent, but these futile efforts will certainly forward the realization of the parent's or helper's own potential as a human being – and isn't this what the journey is about? It is good to remember that love will transform the lover, even if it fails to save the loved one.

Inside My Mother's Shield: The Development of Loyalty and Belonging

Recently, reflecting on the role my mother played in my development, I am amazed about all the times she took my side believing that my intentions were honourable. At about age sixteen, I remember having a boyfriend living in the United States and wanting desperately to keep the connection with him, before he was sent to Viet Nam to defend his country. Confused, I wanted to better understand his commitment to war. There was no MSN, no Facebook and no Internet to shorten the sense of geographical and emotional distance between us. The telephone with the obligatory long distance charges was my only option, Each time that I called, I impulsively gave someone else's phone number to the operator so that my parents would not receive the bill. By the end of that summer, Jack was off to war and I was left to pay a huge phone bill which my mother found out about through an inquiry from Bell Canada.

Mom took my side with Bell Canada, assuring this large corporation that she would take care of it (and me). Mom instinctively knew that it was unnecessary to take a swipe at my dignity by making nasty accusations about what I had done. She told no one, not even my Uncle, about the mistake which I had made. Instead she approached me with a compassionate tone, understanding that my emotional need to call Jack was greater than my cognitive capacity to reason out that there were consequences to making calls using someone else's phone number.

Mom could have accused me of cheating, stealing, and lying and she could have berated me by labeling me a bad girl and an unruly teenager or worse. Instead, she chose to be on my side, to stand up for me when I least expected it and to come alongside me when I needed her most. Putting me in a position of losing face would in her eyes strip me of my dignity. My mom was there for me, knowing that my fragile sense of belonging to her was (for that moment) in her hands. I could have experienced the sting of loneliness and stayed stuck in a state of numbness. Instead, Mom primed my loyalty to her, and I, more than ever, wanted to please her at a time when the direction of my life was tenuous.

Two months later, Jack was killed in Vietnam. I turned to my mother whose arms simultaneously invited me into the dark void of mourning while shielding me from those who minimized my grief and loss.

Had it not been for her incredible
ability to stick up for me without really
knowing whether I was guilty or not, I
might have been stuck in my
woundedness for a lifetime, unable to
form deeper, more intimate
relationships.

An email exchange between Susan and the mother of a 14-year old boy

Susan,

Jerry was bragging to some friends at school that he had a hunting knife in his back pack. This was discovered by the teachers and he was sent to the office. Apparently, he took it (along with another that I found in his room) when he was at his uncle's a week and a half ago. I know Jerry has taken things in the past, and lately he does seem to have an interest in knives. During the time in the office Jerry also disclosed that he had cigarettes and two lighters and claimed he was holding them for someone else.

Jerry got off to a difficult start to school beginning on the first day with peers calling him names and also an incident on the bus with food being thrown at him and more name calling. He had been so excited to return with such high hopes and then after the first day was wanting to quit school. Now he is suspended for an undetermined period of time (at least 5 days); they will confirm how long tomorrow. I understand the concept of the consequences and the seriousness of Jerry's poor judgment but honestly I don't think Jerry meant harm to anyone. I believe they will use Jerry to convey a message to the school - which will likely not result in his favour either.

I am just so uncertain how to proceed and what consequences I should be putting in place at home too. I have already decided that I will need to speak with his uncle and tell him what happened as well as let him know that Jerry will not be able to visit for a while because I do not think it is safe and his uncle is unable to supervise him if he is able to find dangerous objects there. I hope I have given you enough information to give you a good representation of the incident.

I look forward to your assistance,

Marilyn.

Dear Marilyn,

This is an event that needs careful attention and a situation in which you must take the alpha position. Clearly, Jerry's anxiety has ramped up to the next stage which Dr. Neufeld refers to as "doing alarming things"; "alarming himself and others" and "engaging in an extreme sport". It is not uncommon for highly anxious people to find something to give them some relief from the chemistry of anxiety. Lighting lighters, watching fire, carrying knives, fantasies of guns, all give an adrenaline rush which produces a short-term "high" and sense of power. After being bullied this week, I would think that Jerry numbed out and tuned out his feelings and without any intention to harm, felt the power of his adrenaline in displaying the knife. Consequences will NOT help!

Jerry's heart has hardened as a way of not feeling the pain of his week and his ability to have mixed feelings is compromised or non-existent. He cannot make good decisions in this situation. He needs reassurance from you that your relationship is OK and that you know he is the kind of boy who would not deliberately find or make trouble. When we give consequences, suspend kids from school and take away the privileges and objects that are of most value to them, we are using our relationships against our kids. He needs safe emotional relationships right now so that he can soften and be more in charge of his impulses. You could frame it that it is the school's policy that suspension is the punishment but you are certain that there is a teacher or principal relationship that has not been harmed. He needs to know that you love him if he unintentionally caused a problem at school and you love him if he fits into the rules. When schools react with alarming sanctions, the most sensitive of kids are provoked to harden up. It is important that he

not know that you are experiencing any alarm.

Stay calm and carry on.

Hope this helps, Marilyn,

Warmly, Susan.

Making Sense of Senselessness

Still stunned by the Vancouver riot following the Stanley Cup, I am incredulous that youth in London/Manchester have unleashed their shameless energy, destroying parts of their cities and leaving fear in their wake. Robert Fulford wrote in the National Post (August 13, 2011) that youth of today are deprived in a different way than Oliver Twist was in the 1830's. Youth today have food in their bellies, places to live and a political system that supports the choice to not work. He believes this has contributed to the belief that there is a right to riot because there is a right to do whatever one wishes.

Yes, there are many missing parts within the rioters: they lack shame for their senseless acts; they lack any caring and sense of responsibility for the outcome of their actions; they are unable to notice the fear on the faces of those whom have been robbed or hurt and they show no concern for their neighbour.

Rootless and unmoved with no stake in society there is no path for these young people to follow to maturity and reach their full potential. Aimless and without boundaries set by wise elders in their lives, youth between the ages of 14 and their late 20's are present in many communities, including Guelph. Supported by the lyrics in popular music, listeners are validated in their thinking that authority deserves nothing but scorn.

Self control, a sense of self-sacrifice and deep concern for our neighbour cannot be taught. These characteristics are part of development and occur only when the ability to experience both anger and restraint at the same time has been cultivated. All of us are wired for benevolence but not everyone grows inside a safe emotional relationship that will foster the unfolding of ambivalence, management of frustration and impulse control.

To be fully human is to care deeply about people, places and the things that matter in life. Parenting that is built on too much control or too little control often results in children numbing out, tuning out and backing out of relationships that are too much to bear. When not feeling cared for and held emotionally safe, a child's development is compromised. Immaturity is the outcome. With immaturity comes the absence of fear, the absence of shame, the absence of responsibility, and the senselessness of rioting and the presence of boasting about destruction on social media sites.

In my own neighbourhood, I witness the loss of the Good Samaritan, the lack of shame in public intoxication, brazen, sexualized behaviour and the careless use of vulgar music pulsating from a garage located next to a park full of children. What happened to these young people? Lost, without the depth of a strongly rooted emotional relationship, young people will continue to behave like savages until we, the adults who are responsible for them, realize that many young people do not feel safe or connected to anything larger than themselves. The antidote for this kind of destruction lies not in timeouts or consequences but in the determination to hold on to our kids until they can hold on to themselves.

The Emerging Adult

A short article in the *Guelph Mercury* (June 21, 2010, p.A11) describes the new "emerging adult" who is involved in the prolonged transition from adolescence – a phase of development which can last as long as twelve years. "Emerging adult" is a phrase coined by sociologist Christian Smith for his book "Souls in Transition: The religious & spiritual lives of emerging adults."

In a longitudinal research project involving 3,290 individuals who were interviewed twice (at ages 13-17 and again 5 years later) Smith found postponement of marriage and parenting as a key factor contributing to the genesis of this new stage of life. Other factors include: the growth in higher education, extending for many into graduate school; changes in the U.S. and global economies, resulting in careers with less security, more frequent job changes, and the need for ongoing training and education; and the willingness of parents to extend financial and other kinds of support to children in their twenties and thirties.

(A fine overview of the book, the research on which it is based and it's many conclusions can be found at: http://www.catholicsoncall.org/generationbridge/generation-bridge-item/2book-review-souls-transition-christian-smith).

Emerging adults are determined to be free but they do not know what is worth doing with that freedom. *In the midst of this confusion continued parental engagement can be an asset (perhaps counter-intuitively) to help emerging adults find that path to the freedom they so desire. (Italics added)*

Working with Troubled Youth

(Introduction of a presentation to a group of security personnel)

Aggression is one of the oldest and most challenging of human problems and indications are, that in children at least, it is on the rise. Aggressive children are basically stuck between a rock and a hard place: unable to change what counts and too emotionally hardened to come to terms with it. Such youth are inclined to attack when up against things they cannot change. Such youth are also unable to benefit from traditional means of discipline such as correction, confrontation, consequences and isolation. In fact these actually make matters worse. Likewise, attempts to teach anger management, self-control or pro-social skills work best with the kids who need it least and least with the kids who need it most.

The key to making sense of aggression is to get past the violating behaviour to the emotional experience of the youth and to what is missing in the youth's mental processing and functioning.

The objectives of this three-hour seminar are:

. to uncover the psychological roots of aggression problems in youth

.to provide an understanding of why aggression is increasing among children

.to outline six pivotal points of intervention with troubled youth which when applied will not create further damage.

When this job is done by officers who have eyes that see troubled youth differently, we believe that we can actually reduce aggressive behaviours. Instead of invoking counterwill we can draw on kids' good intentions. Often, kids start to see themselves differently, feel safer and are less likely to continue alarming themselves and us.

Bullying

"(They) cannot tolerate the feelings of vulnerability that come together with feelings of caring."

The Bullying Instinct

Humans are born with two important instincts: alpha instincts and dependent instincts. Alpha instincts include the instincts to assume responsibility, to take control, to give direction, to shield and to have the last word. The evolutionary purpose of alpha instincts is to care for the needy, the weak and the vulnerable. Dependent instincts are the exact opposite: to seek help, to follow, to defer, to look up to, to take direction from, to take one's bearings from. These two instincts are meant to be complementary. They are also meant to be fluid: those in the alpha position are meant to move naturally to the dependent position if a stronger alpha appears that can take care of them. The problem occurs when children are wounded emotionally. Such children cannot tolerate the feelings of vulnerability that come together with feelings of caring. The vulnerability is too much to bear, and must be defended against by 'filtering out' feelings of caring and responsibility. The result is that their powerful alpha instincts are now left unchecked and unguided. These instincts are still evoked by displays of weakness and vulnerability in others. However, they become employed for the opposite purpose of exploiting and dominating rather than taking care of.

Alarmed, Aggressive & Lost: Alpha Instincts Gone Bad

Today, September 14th, 2013, the *Globe and Mail's* senior international correspondent, Mark McKinnon, wrote about the tens of thousands of Syrian children who are now living in Jordanian refugee camps after fleeing from the horrors of civil war. There are 130,000 people living there and 50% of them are under the age of 18. He reports that even when these children are playing, their behaviour is aggressive. They hit one another for no reason, they destroy their school materials and they choose violent video games that divide the children into teams which recreate the Regime against the Rebels. Most of the boys in the camps now belong to a gang and the girls, fearing rape, do their best to keep themselves isolated and out of sight.

In his research which untangles the histories of psychology and neurology, Dr. Louis Cozolino (2009) points out that neural networks are burnt in to the brain's neural networks in reaction to real or imagined threats. Understanding the brain requires knowledge of the community context in which the person is embedded. Syrian children, subjected to life threatening incidents for prolonged periods of time, are in a state of hyperarousal during which adrenaline and cortisol (which inhibit decision-making and impulse control) are pumping through their systems. Dr. Gordon Neufeld's developmental, attachment-based paradigm informs us that when the brain is experiencing more stimulation than it can bear, emotional filters in the brain will reduce all vulnerable feelings through a built-in process of numbing out or defendedness. Workers in the refugee camps have noticed that many badly wounded children are unaware of their pain or if they are hungry, happy, sad or in danger. Violence, callousness and brazenness are bred in brains that have lost the emotional capacity for empathy and caring.

A flight from vulnerability leads to a loss of caring and those most defended against their wounds are likely to wound others. Both the atrocities in Syria and the aggressive gang behaviour among youth in the Jordanian refugee camps are escalating as separation and the context of attachment disappears.

Emotionally wounded children also live in our own community. The evidence of separation from those to whom they should be attached is much more subtle than in Syria. There is a whole new society of youth which lacks an extended family to provide multiple attachments. Children are sourced out to programs in which they are to acquire life skills. Unless they are attached to the person providing the skills, the risk is high that peers (along with the peers' lack of life experience) will matter most and the epidemic of immaturity will grow.

Children no longer talk about their feelings; parents and teachers are afraid of a child's emotionality. Saying "I miss you" is interpreted as neediness and activities trump feeling safe in relationship. Today's youth are 40% less like to show empathy than the youth of previous generations (Konrath et al, 2011). In a large study, the US National Institute of Health reported that one-third of children had been bullied within the four week period prior to being interviewed. One in two female university students is sexually assaulted before graduation. Children are more exposed to the main source of wounding which is peer interaction. Social networking now means that school interactions never end and that children are increasingly socializing in environments where adults are not able to protect them (Neufeld 2013).

Kids are turning against their siblings, divorced parents openly continue to fight in front of their offspring and Facebook has become the bathroom wall of the past (Neufeld 2013). Alpha children are losing their caring instinct and the instinct to bully takes over.

Demanding, prescriptive, bossy, oppositional, ridiculing, annoying, irritating and loathing, the bully asserts dominance by exploiting another's needs.

Unlike the Jordanian refugee camps full of lost, unattached, emotionally and physically wounded Syrian children, we can step back into the lives of our children and help them to regain their feelings, however painful they may be. From the caring alpha adults in their lives, our kids can receive what they need to reach their full potential and to fit into society. Syrian kids and their traumatized parents (if they have living parents at all) have no options for caring. Full of revenge, going back to Syria to join the *jihad* is the only option they can comprehend. Lost, with no safe attachments, their alpha instincts have gone bad. All that matters is the war. There is no fear of death, nor of pain, nor of hurt.

Take back your kids with your own caring alpha position. YOU matter. Safe emotional relationships are capable of rebuilding dysfunctional neural structures through the healing energy of secure attachment.

Fighting against Bullying

The current "attack" on bullying, employing legislation, celebrity visits to schools, mass rallies in schools and ribbon-and-shirt campaigns will, in all likelihood fail in the same way that Stop Smoking and Safe Sex campaigns fail. These methods are directed at the bullying behaviour but the source of bullying is not the behaviour it's the psychology of the bully. The bully is simply behaving according to the dictates of his/her bullying instincts which involve a combination of a need to dominate combined with an inability to care.

The need to dominate (to be "alpha") is found in all species and there's likely not much we can do about it; but the ability to care is related to how vulnerable the bully feels. The more vulnerable a person is, the less the ability to care for others. Every piece of research – now involving tens of thousands of students in studies around the world – concludes the same thing: students feel less vulnerable when they are in regular contact with at least one caring adult. The solution to bullying isn't a mass rally; it's the regular presence of a caring parent, grandparent, teacher, or mentor to whom our children and youth can feel attached. This is how you unmake a bully.

Significance and Bullying

Neufeld argues that there are six roots of attachment: sensory, sameness, belonging/loyalty, significance, love and being known. While it is true that all of the roots can feed one another, and be part of one another the need for significance can – if we choose to – be viewed on its own independent of other needs and wants (roots). Professor Robert Kegan, a human development psychologist at Harvard, talked about the ability to "recruit" others – by voice, eye contact, touch – so that our needs can be met. Clearly, if others do not see us, do not regard us as being needy or as a person who is distinguishable from other objects in the environment, then we will have no significance for them. This is significance at the level of existence, not just the significance which is defined as importance, but significance defined as "being".

To be significant – to be seen, to be experienced by others – we need to be not only present to them but also available to them. They need to be able to interact with us. They need to be able to react to us as well as being able to reach out to us. Karen Horney talked about moving towards or moving against others in order to make contact. She also talked about moving away from others. When we move away from others without having made

connection or without having created or experienced any form of attachment to them then there is no hope of significance.

To move towards others we must risk. We risk having them move against us or move away from us. It may even be risky if they move towards us – for then we have the challenge and the opportunity to connect with them, to form an attachment. If we are open to these possibilities then we can become significant to others. However, what happens when we are not open to others, when attachment to them is seen as something to be avoided either because we fear what they might do or because we are not certain what we can or might do? To avoid these unknown or feared outcomes we may become defended, perhaps even detached. Recruitment – absolutely vital for the infant - becomes potentially dangerous/anathema.

The defended individual still participates in the human drama in which contact with others is part of the human script. But, movement towards is likely too risky; movement away further isolates and distresses the individual; movement against – bullying – becomes the modus operandi. The quest to exist, to matter, to be of significance becomes so anxiety-provoking that contact takes on aggressive forms – some overt and

obvious – some subtle and barely
noticeable, but they all serve the same
protective function.

The old Transactional Analysis mantra,
"I'm OK – You're OK" can be translated
"I am significant – You are significant"
and the movement is towards others
and attachment. The defended form
of this, it's obverse, becomes "The
closest I can come to being significant
is to be experienced as someone who
hurts or rejects you" and in this there is
no attachment.

Subtleties in the Making and Unmaking of a Bully: Uncovering the Family System

In their differences and conflicts, in their endless inherent imperfections, all families are a strange system of competitive dynamics between the self and the whole. Must one person always win?

If we understood this dynamic, we could more effectively undcover the antecedents that lead up to creating a bully. Abuse of power among siblings, between parents or between parents and their children poisons growth. Using a power holding position to achieve results does not recognize the difference between respect and fear. Eye-rolls, sarcasm, put-downs (disguised as humour), teasing, shaming, pulling the wool over someone's eyes, exploiting a person's fears in order to belittle or control them, taking away a prized activity or article (consequencing), making fun of, withdrawal (time-outs) and silence are all based in competition as one person tries to position him/herself as better or more powerful than the other. Anxiety, fear and agitation often emerge from stressful situations in families and fuel the appetite of the bully. In this anxious world, everyone has the potential to become that which is despised. Over-reactive stress response systems push us to protect ourselves by closing off parts of our lives that leave us feeling vulnerable. We numb ourselves to what we sense threatens us. We defend ourselves inside a safe womb of eating, drinking, medicating, shopping and attaching to technology, all contexts that will filter out the feelings that make us feel vulnerable. By numbing out, the ability to care, to show compassion and to form meaningful relationships are also lost.

Culture has changed. Vulnerability is seen as a weakness, fearlessness is admired and perfection is a goal. Blocking out fear, anxiety, shame and disappointment also eliminates any experience of joy, love, belonging and hope. The bully is numbed out, tuned out and has backed out of relationships. The bully has beaten vulnerability to the punch and cannot be in touch with his or her own emptiness. By numbing out the dark emotions, there is no ability to let oneself soften into caring about, showing respect or loving another.

Embracing vulnerability and imperfection with unconditional acceptance will help families to see each other with new eyes. Caring, compassion and consideration will trump shaming, blaming and complaining. Relationships will become what we strive for because it will be safe to uncover our authentic selves. Bullying will become extinct because of the emotional generosity afforded to each individual in the family system.

Acceptance of small and large annoyances, respect for one another, a sense of sameness, belongingness, loyalty, importance and love will prevail. The bully will be understood inside and out and with that knowingness be unmade and then cultivated to reach his full potential. Everyone in the system wins!

Child Development

"There is no way to know children if we are doing something else."

A Therapist's Lament

Yesterday, I watched a little eleven week old boy sweeping his eyes across my clients' faces, seeking approving eyes and looking for signs of contact. When I was allowed to hold him looking into his eyes, smiling with warmth, delight and approval, he would smile back at me. I watched him with his new mom and her husband (his foster parents, hopefully adoptive parents in one year) engaged in the same ritual, of watching for "the look of love".

The little guy's alarm parameters are in chaos. He will visit his bio parents twice a week for one year (mandated); less, if before the year is up they decide they want someone to adopt him. On each visit he is unaccompanied in a car with an agency-approved driver. He is alone in the back seat of an unfamiliar car on his way to a supervised visit (this means that a social worker takes notes of what she observes) at Family and Children's Services (FCS). He is sobbing and grieving those eyes of delight, the warmth of the arms of those who care for him the majority of the time, the sound of the reassuring voices, and the pitter-patter of a loving three-year old brother's voice. He is swept off with only the familiar scents he carries on his blanket. The relationships which he absolutely depends on are threatened

and off he goes to be further alarmed inside a protocol that is endorsed by FCS and has the blessing of both our provincial and national governments.

Both of his bio-parents are former street people, developmentally stuck and depressed. Each has a biochemical makeup which is the product of two generations of involvement with the FCS system. Their lives have been lived out within concentric circles of despairing stories. The FCS system is mired in outdated policies and failed strategies. Neither the system nor the bio-parents are able to give the warmth, delight and enjoyment for which he is searching. For the two nights following a visit he is up all night looking, searching, scanning for his new mom's eyes. She settles him, holds him, rocks him until he falls asleep in her arms, accepting that he will wake-up crying. She continues to give him more than what he is looking for and needs, knowing that the cycle will start again next visit, three days later.

The first face he saw was that of his frightened, depressed and anxious biological mother. His brain's alarm circuitry was activated. His attachment alarm diminishes in the presence of warmly supportive adults but is triggered twice a week when he experiences his distanced biological parents. He will ride this emotional wave until a system which is completely uninformed sanctions an adoption by parents (my clients) who will work hard to provide the safe context in which both neurogenesis and development can happen. In this FCS system the needs (and "rights") of the bio-parents trump the requirements of a developing baby.

There is hope for this child. He is being given what he needs: complete safety. My prayer is that his developmental needs can be met inside his new family's womb of attachment so that he won't become so preoccupied with feeling cortisol and adrenalin that he becomes anxious, agitated and then starts doing alarming things to both fill his attachment fuel tank and feed his biochemical need to be in alarm. My hope is that my clients (within their entire family supportive circle) can facilitate the rebuilding of his willingness to attach through their cues of unconditional acceptance (warmth and understanding - no matter what).

Are We Pushing Independence Too Soon?

While rocking my grandson, his head nestled up under my chin, his hand winding my hair through his fingers, my eyes filled with tears as we both enjoyed the warmth of the fireplace behind us. There is a wind of change blowing across the Ontario Educational System which will invite my grandson to start school next September. Born in late December, he will have all the rights and privileges to become a student before his fourth birthday.

The image is that full-day kindergarten will provide children with opportunities to improve their social skills, their mental health and academic performance. As an early health enhancement program, the goal is to provide an early childhood curriculum which will deliver better nutrition, more physical exercise and cognitive stimulation. This is intended to ensure equal opportunities for achievement.

How could this trusting little soul snuggled safely on my lap have a government imposed plan suggesting that he can be sculpted into a desired form? Doesn't the new system understand that there are seasons in a child's development? Substance comes before form, desire comes before discipline and integrity before charity.

As a developmentalist, I his grandmother, understand that there is much work to be done in the natural unfolding of his developmental process. He needs care and nourishing so that his feelings won't become lost in sea of alarm and then get turned off.

The provision of kindergarten and day-care opportunities will do nothing towards cultivating safe environments where there is room for children to grow. Jonas Himmelstrand, addressing the Swedish parliament in December, 2008 commented, "Swedish family policies during the last 30 years have resulted in insecure children and youth, stressed adults and lower quality parenthood. As security in children is a strong social legacy, it is a negative spiral." It is the parents, teachers, caregivers, child-care workers and educational assistants in this new initiative, who have the power to grow our kids up to their full potential. Adults in the equation must be willing and able to attend to and to protect the child; to help the child to feel safe and accepted, no matter what.

Children who can rest from worrying if their caregivers like them, who can rest from having to make too many decisions for themselves, who can rest from being pushed and pressured into busyness will be the ones who have a space carved out for them in which their own self will unfold.

As for my grandson, he will stay at home with his parents and grandparents for an extra year and through his dependency on us find a path to responsibility taking, independence and becoming an individual. Instead of filling up his time with activities intended to enrich his life, we will create psychological room so that he can find his initiative, creativity and originality.

I yearn for all those parents (who cannot provide this luxurious state in which their child can unfold naturally) to make it their mission to focus on the power of relationship in keeping their child both emotionally and physically safe. A child who is fearful and who does not feel safe, will find a way to survive by numbing out his/her feelings. A child without fear is a child who will become independent too soon and orient to his peers. Ultimately this is the path of growing old without growing up.

Boredom – a Brief Perspective

From a developmentalist's point of view, boredom is stressful, unsettling and dysregulating. My sense is that boredom is a function of the brain's maturation stage. If emergence, adaptability and integration have not happened, the brain is differentiated without being integrated. The neural fibers haven't grown between the upstairs brain (planning, organizing and executing competencies) and the downstairs brain (feelings) triggered by the amygdala which is being teased by implicit memories (memories without words).

We can help our kids move out of their feelings of boredom (imagine sitting on the hub of a wheel) by moving them to the rim of the wheel where there are more options for feelings and experiences of themselves. This is done by addressing - through story telling - some of the things kids experienced in the past and helping them to make their memories explicit. Feelings with words and stories attached are much easier to live with than the itch of implicit memories which cause the brain to numb out leaving the child with no capacity to find another way.

When a child says: "I am bored", s/he may be seeking an engaging moment or a time of connection with those who are important to him/her. Boredom can also be an opportunity to point out your child's good intentions by saying: "I bet if you sit beside me here quietly for a few minutes, your good brain will sort through all of your files and find something that will satisfy it".

The "Orchid Hypothesis"

(Here it is a synopsis of a Toronto Globe and Mail article found at: http://www.theglobeandmail.com/news/opinions/editorials/the-school-of-fewer-hard-knocks/article1458553/)

There has been an explosion of research surrounding the concept of "orchid children". It is at the intersection of attachment theory and genetics and there is a helpful metaphor which can be used to picture the situation. In a field of dandelions, most of which have normal genetic make-up, most can survive a wide range of difficult conditions; they carry a protective gene that makes them trauma-resistant. There are two variations of this gene (called *alleles*) which greatly magnify the risk of perishing when the environment or the soil becomes too hostile for them. The exciting findings of the new research is that if the dandelions with these two alleles are given special treatment – nurtured and protected – one group will do about as well as the "normal" dandelions but the other will bloom and not only catch up to the rest of the field but surpass it. They will show resilience and development in excess of what their cousins demonstrate.

Apparently, the same situation holds true for children. Some overly sensitive children who might exhibit a variety of stress-related disorders and who are prone to acting out will, with the nurturance of strong attachment, develop and mature without showing long-term effects of trauma. Others, who start out with the same hypersensitivity, given the same attachment and the same special treatment from caring adults, will show development and maturation which is greater than either the average group or the others in the hypersensitive group.

In the past, we thought of hypersensitivity as being a liability, as a condition which left the child too vulnerable to trauma. Now, it appears as though some of these hypersensitive children – the orchids – will not only be protected from trauma but will also thrive, be creative and curious, and will avoid the behavioural and emotional problems which beset their peers – these are the dandelions.

Reclaiming Our Children

We are trying to do all the right things for our kids but recent University of Minnesota research points out that young children spend more time in cars going to and from activities than they do sitting at the dinner table, involved in the simple ritual of the family meal. By trying to give our kids everything, we have overlooked the importance of surrendering ourselves to the art and science of building and sustaining a relationship with them.

With all good intentions, following the advice of experts, we have managed to cut ourselves off from our kids and thrust them into activities to fill them up. Working with parents, coaches and teachers, I am learning that many adults are so anxious about doing "the wrong thing" that we have become paralyzed. The contradictory advice which has been offered to parents over the past thirty years has contributed to the confusion about what to do. Looking for a one-size-fits-all theory, parents buy into one approach only to find in a short time that there is another theory which has superseded the last one.

Theory has proven to be ineffectual. The modern self-esteem industry which basically tells every child that they are "special" just for "being a person" has become just as hollow as tough love, consequences, time-outs and rewards. Medicating, punishing, providing alibis (diagnoses) for "spoiled" and "undisciplined children" hasn't made a difference either.

Parents, teachers, counsellors and child-care providers are stretched to the limit. We do spend more time with our kids than in past generations but when we look at what we are doing during this time, a troubling picture unfolds. Often, it seems we are engaged in parallel but separate activities. Mother may be supervising her five-year-old's supper while simultaneously arranging a meeting for the next day; brother is e-mailing several friends while talking with yet another friend on the phone; Dad is looking up from his computer every ten minutes or so to say to whomever will listen, "It's almost bedtime!"..

There is no way to get to know children if we are doing something else. I remember clearly, many years ago, one of my children walking over to where I was, down on my hands and knees, washing a floor. Carefully, he put his hand on my shoulder, bent over to look into my eyes and asked timidly, "When can you stop being so busy and just talk to 'your little boy'?".. This was a heartfelt response from my son who was desperate to be seen, heard, and touched, to feel that he mattered, that

he belonged to me, that I loved him
and that he was truly known by me.

When children aren't in relationship
with an adult who wants to know them
inside out, and to protect them from
all the expectations burdening them,
there will always be something else to
fill the dark void. Parents, teachers and
caregivers are floundering are
floundering in their own moral
confusion but it doesn't have to stay
that way; relationships relationships
are the answer.

Sarah's Emergence

To-day we are caring for our neighbour's daughter, Sarah. The toy doctor's bag is off the shelf and in full use. She has transformed our upstairs into a physician's office. Glasses set purposefully on her nose, stethoscope around her neck, she instructs us (my adult daughter and myself) to take our place in the waiting-room. We do so. Yes, we do her bidding. Sarah is in her alpha mode trying to make sense of an accident that befell her grandmother. Demonstrating her viability in this moment, she has categorized herself as the "Doctor", the knower, the one who has the answers. She feels guilt about keeping us waiting when her preference is to cure us instantaneously. Sarah is full of herself in the best way possible. She is vital, full of ideas and coming from a place of being in charge of the direction of her energy. She sees her existence as one of utmost importance as she undertakes this quest to figure things out (about broken hips) by herself. For a few moments, through her play, Sarah is releasing her attachment needs and venturing forth as a separate human being and showing us signs of her viability.

Stanley Greenspan's concept of structuring "floor time" describes ways to support a child's intellectual, emotional, and physical development through interactive play. He suggests a child's growth is promoted by simply following her lead and joining in! By playfully relating to the child, the parent is helping to incorporate learning experiences into the child's developmental profile thereby enriching the depth and range of a child's thinking and emotions as they venture forth. Nowhere in his work, could I find a reference to attachment needs being fulfilled as the precursor to this emergent process. I would have missed the developmental richness of Sarah's play without the Neufeld paradigm and the vocabulary with which I could describe what my eyes were seeing.

One at a time, she calls out a name and then apologizes for "the wait". After leading one of us into her operatory (her bedroom at our house), and thanking the (imaginary) paramedics for their swift delivery, she gives an instruction to lie down on the bed so that she can "have a look at that nasty broken hip". With great gentleness, she straddle sits across her patient's legs and proclaims that with a little surgery she can "fix that hip – better than new". She is confident that she has the answer for the brokenness. Without anesthetic, but with some quick maneuvering, the hip is fixed and the patient is off to rehabilitation.

Sarah finishes her work with the patient and then sheds her tears of futility. There was nothing she could do to prevent the accident. Through her emergent play, she is able to move out of the alpha position and back into her dependent place in the hierarchy asking for "big hugs and good food".

I now understand how evidence of Sarah's emergence through her play has brought her to a place of adaptation after registering the futility of trying to change the impossible. This is one of many singular experiences that will unfold as she matures. The essence of integration is yet to come, when she is developmentally ready. She is finding herself.

Separation and the Attachment Brain in Children Ages 2 to 8

The combination of child development and attachment theories provides an understanding of how parental interactions with their children influence the developmental pathways pre-wired in the brain. The mind develops as the genetically programmed maturation of the brain responds to ongoing experience.

Attachment experiences enable children to thrive and achieve an adaptive capacity for balancing their emotions, thinking and empathic connections with others. The latest work in neuroscience suggests that attachment relationships are likely to promote the development of the integrative capacities of the brain.

Dr. Gordon Neufeld's work in child development psychology and attachment points out that the brain is designed to take care of the development of the fundamental foundations for normal development. We as parents just need to provide the context for development to take hold.

How do we do this? By holding our children in close proximity to us and by providing interactive and reflective experiences we begin the process of putting down the roots of attachment. Protecting children from the experience of separation that they are not yet ready to experience or helping children to experience their feelings of alarm when separation is unavoidable. Unfortunately, being laughed at, picked on, not being chosen for the team, rejection, mommy going to work (and the list goes on) are all part of life's experiences.

There are resolutions to separation problems. As parents we can protect our child as long as possible from sensing his or her inherent insecurity by not showing movies that have something bad that happens to the characters. Disney movies are often constructed on the theme of separation and loss.

Replacing alarm-based discipline such as warnings, threats, raising the voice, intimidation, 1-2-3 magic and time-outs with simple rules, structure and routine will solicit good behaviour and reduce feelings of separation.

Entry into child-care or the school system is a time of high separation anxiety for both parents and children. Taking time to meet the teacher before school starts and demonstrating attachment behaviours such as eye contact, smiling and nodding to each other in front of our child paves the way for passing the baton of attachment. Research will get underway early this fall to test the effectiveness of taking a match-making approach with teachers at school entry.

We can also start with separations that are easy to face like spending time in a reading group while mommy and daddy watch from across the room. Demonstrating our own confidence in the child that s/he can handle the separation that we are helping her to face.

As parents we can also help our children to develop other ways of holding on to us while they are at school or in a child-care program. A small article of our clothing, a special symbol of our love, a picture of the two of us together can be attachment replacements that are sometimes enough to help a child to start a new activity without mommy or daddy.

Gently and gradually helping our child to come to terms with something they can't have or where loss is unavoidable will involve allowing our children to have their tears. It is important that we not get in the way of these tears since they are the brain's way of helping our children to become resilient.

With this carefully created context of attachment, children are able to develop the courage to endure the feelings of alarm while still being able to go for what it is that they want to do (perhaps going to a gymnastics class or playing soccer in an organized league).

Holding us close is a pre-eminent need of our children. It is more eminent than hunger. Parents are the active sculptors of their children's brains. Family experiences create shape, depth and breadth in the development of neural pathways.

Counterwill in an Adolescent Boy

(Feedback to a Neufeld Directed Studies Program student)

Dear Jill

This case study is one of the finest that I have read. Clearly, you have fully integrated the Neufeld paradigm into your work. Lucky Jerry to have you walk the maze beside him, while taking him to a place where he can experience the fullness of life. Yes, trusting the process, priming the pump and standing by to enjoy the maturation that springs forth is a joy to behold. You have given this young man a chance to reach his full potential. Your hard work has paid off.

Your section on Counterwill could be stretched out a little. When Jerry came to you his appetite for autonomy, for being his own person was hidden behind the expectations his parents held for him. His counterwill (procrastination) was indeed his resistance to being told what to do. This comes from a desire to know his own mind. The more conscious he became of what his mom and dad wanted the more resistant he became. Their demands were greater than his desires. He was demonstrating his intrinsic sense that he needed to push their agendas out of the way so that he could find his own. Unconsciously, Jerry was countering the will of adults in charge so that he could emerge as a separate being. My sense is that you worked with his parents to make way for his preferences. Each time his parents impose their will the more it will backfire.

Often, as therapists, we need to push parents out of the way to make way for their child's agendas. Seeing this window of opportunity, you aligned yourself with the counterwill, moving the symptoms of alarm out of the way and saw that it was Jerry's counterwill that was protecting him from outside direction and influence from those to whom he was not attached. You gave Jerry a place to get to know his own mind so that he could mange critical incidents in both the present and the future (father collapsing etc.).

I encourage you to look at the positive implications of Jerry's counterwill. Without counterwill, none of us would ever mature.

A wonderful testament to the power of the Neufeld paradigm.

Terrible Two's and Saying "No"!

(Re: "Terrible Two? That's when kids 'no' more (a reaction to Drew Edwards' column, Guelph Mercury, August, 2010)

Drew Edwards' column referring to the *"Terrible Twos? That's when kids 'no' more"* seems to be written from a somewhat harassed parent and is apparently intended to illuminate, or perhaps to entertain. This response is intended to both support and inform those who care for our toddlers. As parents, grandparents and child care providers, we must think very carefully about how to interpret and then respond to a two-year old who says "no". On the one hand, children need us to script the rules in order to be safe. On the other hand, when a child says "no" this is part of early brain development and is *absolutely necessary* to counter feelings of being pressured or tricked into doing something which is directed by someone else's will.

Saying "no" serves a very important developmental purpose. Growing one's own will is a great resource for living. Being able to stand up for oneself, having both the passion to know what one wants in life and the drive to go for it are wired within the developing brain. It's not that the child is "strong-willed" or that the Free Will switch has been activated. It actually takes a life-time to develop a strong will and children are at the very beginning of the process. Hearing "no" from a child can give us hope that s/he is developing as nature intended. It can also be a warning sign that we have some work to do inside the relationship.

Understanding the developing brain of your immature child will help you to parent from a place of confidence and competence. Your journey has just begun! May you cultivate a rich relationship with your child so that s/he can reach his/her full human potential. For more insights on parenting, I refer you to Dr. Gordon Neufeld's book: *Hold On To Your Kids.*

The Craving Spot

In the Business Section of the November 10-17, 2008 edition of MacLean's magazine there is an article with the heading: *CAUTION: do not read this story*. Of course, my heart started racing and I just had to read it. The following is my brief summary of the content.

The newest brain research has focused on an area called the "craving spot". When it is activated, we feel powerless to stop what we are doing. One of the best ways to activate this spot is to tell someone they shouldn't do something or to stop doing what they are already doing. This research (using more than 2,000 volunteers) shows that scare techniques ("Smoking Kills!".) or campaigns such as "Just Say No!"., or "Practice Safe Sex" may be exactly what the brain needs to get active and to pursue the wrong course of action.

Finally, some science to back both the Bloom County cartoon Gordon uses in his Counterwill presentation and what all of us who work with children experience every day.

The Downside of Alcohol, Marijuana, Substances and SSRIs

All experience is learning. Any activity that brings success increases the neurotransmitter dopamine which promotes the desire to seek risks, reward and motivation. All drugs including SSRIs like Paxil and Luvox increase the production of dopamine while at the same reduces that of serotonin. Drugs and alcohol trick the brain's dopamine (reward) system.

Boredom is an indication that the teen is defended against feelings of vulnerability. When defended we don't look at our own mistakes, don't miss the people whom we care for and we actually experience 80% fewer feelings. When bored or defended, the teen looks for things to do to increase dopamine (motivation) and reduce serotonin (thereby reducing any sense of satiation and/or inhibition) in the system. In other words, when the teen feels empty, s/he will look for something that feels fulfilling (email, Facebook, texting, alcohol or marijuana use or prescriptions for SSRIs) so that s/he will avoid vulnerable feelings especially depression. SSRIs, alcohol and marijuana soothe but also block fulfillment. Substance abuse messes up the scoring system in the brain. Production of dopamine and serotonin become mismatched and confused.

Substances (marijuana, alcohol and SSRIs) blunt emotions and dopamine activity is reduced. People who are prescribed SSRI's are less likely to feel the intense dopamine driven feelings of romantic love and sorrow of loss, both of which are universal experiences designed by nature to cultivate robust souls who can adapt to the ups and downs of living. Life is hard!!!!

The Teen Brain

Hypothesis: Incomplete brains account for emotional problems and irresponsible behaviour in teens.

Research in 1991 at the University of Arizona reviewed past research on teens in 186 pre-industrial societies. One of the important conclusions they drew about these cultures was that 60% had no word for adolescence! These were the societies in which teens spent almost all of their time with adults. In these contexts, the teens showed almost no signs of psychopathology and anti-social behaviour. In some of the cultures any psychopathology which did exist was only mild.

In the U.S. the peak age for most arrests is about age 18. American parents and teens are in conflict with one another 20 times a month (a great source of pain for both). Another extensive study in 2004 suggests that 18 is the peak age for depression. Drug use is high in this cohort, as is violent crime. American schools have a police presence and our Canadian schools are hiring community officers to keep schools safe. High school drop-out rates are high in both countries.

What's going on here? It seems we are forcing our youth to break away from adults; rather than teaching them to become adults. All our restrictions at home, in the schools and in the community are separating our youth into a culture of their own. This is not happening in Eastern European countries.

We know from the research in neuroscience that our teens use their prefrontal cortex differently than do adults. Sleep studies indicate that there is a decline in delta (deep sleep) activity during teen years which might support our observations that there are fewer interconnections happening among the neurons.

Other studies suggest that the prefrontal cortex is not fully developed until the mid-twenties. This planning and executive functioning part of the brain is immature, yet we are expecting that our teens are capable of making important decisions that impact their futures without our participation.

Is it any wonder that in the teen culture, our adolescents try not to feel. For the most part, many of us have tried to protect our children from feeling any sadness about the things in their lives they cannot change. Poor marks must be the fault of poor teaching; not being first in the piano recital is because the judge was weak; difficulty with friends is because the friends are mean and the list goes on.

Grieving is part of life. To mature is to discover one's own resilience. When our children are diverted from feeling their sadness about the losses and failures that life brings their way, their ability to adapt is compromised. Adaptation can only occur when children are allowed to find their feelings of futility. Once futility is experienced and the loss or disappointment is integrated, resilience develops. If resilience is not present, immaturity prevails.

Children who are most at risk are those who are entering puberty prematurely, sometimes as early as ages eight to ten. These children are often still immature and dependent because they are not attached deeply/ vulnerably to their parents. The more rooted a child is in the attachment to their parents, the more likely the child will receive the love, support and nurturing necessary to endure pubescence. Without those roots, the less likely the child will be able to shoe-horn into society successfully.

At any age, when there is a void in the attachment with parents, our children will find a substitute. This substitute is peer culture. Peers are not agents of socialization. Adults are! Yet, we have courted the peer culture for our children. At school, we teach peer mediation so that kids can negotiate conflicts with other kids. Sleep-overs,

taking a child's friend on vacation with the family and leaving our children to do their homework with friends are only a few of the ways we have encouraged our children to put their friends ahead of us.

We need to hold onto our children so we are aware of the impediments that are getting in the way of their development into maturity. If we take our children off the developmental map or push them into situations they are incapable of handling, we risk losing them to their vulnerability. Creating a context for relationships in which we hold onto our natural authority is possible if we follow our instincts. The prefrontal cortex of our teens will mature according to the genetic map which is pre-wired in the brain.

Another huge brain structure, the corpus callosum, connects the left (logical) brain to the right (emotional) brain. This structure is still growing during the teen years. We expect our teens to make sense of their feelings and their thoughts without the benefit of the completion of the highway that sends messages back and forth between right and left hemispheres of the brain.

These young people are unable to understand paradox or to hold two feelings at the same time. Their intentions to perform a task may be voiced but the motivation to do the necessary work to follow through and to complete the task is not there. These children do not experience any inner conflict. They are unable to say, "If I study this material and do my homework, I will be in a better position to pass. If I don't do the required work, I will probably fail". Logical consequences are not part of their world view.

Tests indicate that between ages 13 and 15 intelligence peaks and that this cohort has the ability to learn new things very quickly. Emotional intelligence is struggling behind. Our teens need us to provide the context so that learning and full emotional development can happen.

Today, our teens are being burped out into a peer culture. Never have there been more suspensions from school, more separation from parents via consequences, grounding and tough love strategies. Look around, there are teens everywhere trying to learn how to become adults but they are trying to learn to do this from one another. In many ways, we expect our kids to know how to do this automatically but we also know intuitively that teens can only learn how to become an adult from those who are responsible for them.

We must hold onto our kids until they can hold onto themselves.

When Your Child Says "No!".: Why Kids Resist

If you have a child who disobeys, defies, talks back, works to rule, does the opposite of what is expected, breaks the rules, becomes preoccupied with taboos or withholds cooperation, please read on. As parents, we must think very carefully about how to respond to a child who says "no".

On the one hand, children do need to hear the rules and understand boundaries in order to be safe and to get along socially. On the other hand, a child's saying "no" is a part of early brain development and is absolutely necessary to counter feelings of being pressured or tricked into doing something which is directed by someone else's will. The child's drive to resist also serves attachment by protecting the child from outside direction and influence. For a child, it simply doesn't feel right to do something for a person with whom he is **not** in relationship.

Saying "no" (counterwill) serves a very important developmental purpose. Growing one's own will is a great life resource. Being able to stand up for oneself, having both the passion to know what one wants in life and the drive to go for it are wired within the developing brain. This prepares the

child to function independently. It's **not** that the child is strong-willed. It actually takes a life-time to develop a strong will and children are at the very beginning of this period.

A child who becomes compliant suffers in later life from not having developed a separate self. Adapting to the needs and feelings of others can only come through sacrificing what a child wants and feels for him/herself. If a child is too frightened to protest or is afraid love will be withdrawn, he will obey at the high cost of unhealthy development and will direct his energy toward his peers as he grows older. When attachment energy is directed toward peers, the context for parenting is destroyed.

When there are relationship or attachment problems counterwill arises. Children want to be good for the people with whom they are attached but when there is no attachment the desire to be good can turn into the impulse to be bad. Whenever children are not attached or in a safe relationship with the adults who are responsible for them (this can happen several times a day), defiance, oppositionality and disobedience flow. It is not intentional; it is related to natural brain impulses.

When our children get stuck in their "no's", we usually start pushing; when our children feel pushed , they put on the brakes; and when our children get further stuck in their resistance, we frequently become stuck in our persistence.

Understanding the developing brain of our immature child will help us to parent from a place of confidence and competence. Hearing a "no" from a child can give us hope that they are developing as they should or it can gives us a warning sign that we have work to do inside the relationship.

Crying and Guilt

"For a child, crying is a way to beckon the caregiver to help regulate their mood or their negative arousal."

Crying and Guilt: A Question for Dr. Neufeld

Gordon, I have been walking around the paradigm this afternoon in two different pairs of shoes. The first pair are my new ones which you gave me during the Master Class so that I could navigate guilt and the other pair are old worn out ones that are searching for how crying fits the Developmental 3D Analysis (see Appendix B).

Here is what I am discovering. I realize that crying is an instinctual relationship behaviour or a way to help us get close. We cry because we need connection with our caregivers in order to accept and heal from pain. In attachment, crying is not about what we let out but whom we let in. The experience of crying is rooted in early childhood and people's relationship with their primary caregiver. We know that those whose parents were attentive, soothing their cries when needed, tend to find that crying gives them solace as an adult. Those whose parents held back or became irritated or overly upset by the child's crying have more difficulty soothing themselves as adults (Alan Schore, 2001).

For a child, crying is a way to beckon the caregiver to help regulate their mood or their negative arousal. As a therapist, I can see that for adults, crying can reflect their level of attachment. Crying can recharge and rebalance internal equilibrium through human connection or can cause withdrawal, shame or guilt.

People in alarm often appear un-affected and say nothing when in fact they are confused, frightened and disturbed by their instincts. Crying is a vulnerable experience which can only be tolerated by those whose parents made room for tears. As you say Gordon; "Whatever a mother cannot invite into existence for herself, she cannot invite in her child".

A good cry is restorative and creative, cleansing although paradoxically it is about pain and relief; despair and hope; agony and comfort; loss and connection, and separation and proximity. Crying makes us viable as individuals. Crying helps us to recover from the bad things that happen to us, things that don't go our way and to weather losses and to give us the resilience to move on to new attachments. No matter how good a cry is we cannot undo loss and pain, bring back a lover nor take back an unintentional stinging remark. Crying helps us to endure our deep ambivalence about intimacy and closeness and to live with that which we cannot change.

I can see that crying is an inborn attachment behaviour designed to protect survival in infancy and social connections later in life. My sense is that guilt has a lot to do with priming attachment behaviour and that crying is a lubricant.

Crying is Inevitable

Re: "Crying is inevitable" (a reaction to Brianne Colchetti's column, *Guelph Mercury*, June 18, 2012).

Oh dear, how unfortunate that in 2012 with all the current research in neuroscience available with a click of a mouse, that an article by a misinformed writer for the Guelph Mercury has an article that promotes sleep training and ferberizing young children. Ferber's work in solving children's sleep problems is almost 40 years old and has been proven harmful to the development of children through the work of Dr. Allan Schore, a respected neuroscientist at UCLA. In fact, Dr. Gabor Mate, in 2006, wrote in one of his weekly. Globe and Mail columns some common sense advice: "A baby cries to express her deepest need -- emotional and physical contact with the parent. The deceptive convenience of Ferberization (sleep training) is one more way in which our society fails the needs of the developing child". Both Schore's work and Mate's insights tell us that the implicit message an infant receives from having her cries ignored is that the world which is represented by her caregivers -- is indifferent to her feelings. Is "sleep training" the framework from which bullying is manifested?

Seeing Through Tears

Notes on: "Seeing Through Tears: Crying and Attachment (2005)", Judith Kay Nelson Ph.D.

The experience of crying is rooted in early childhood and people's relationship with their primary caregiver. The outcome of Nelson's doctoral work points out that those whose parents were attentive and who soothed their cries when needed, tend to find that crying gives solace as an adult. Those whose parents held back or became irritated or overly upset by the child's crying have more difficulty soothing themselves as adults. For a child, crying is a way to beckon the caregiver, and to regulate mood or negative arousal. Those who grow up unsure of when or whether that soothing is available get stuck in protest crying. These individuals cannot work through their grief if they are stuck in protest crying (tears of frustration) are hard to soothe and can't do anything to undo their early loss. Nelson states that sad crying across the lifespan is an appeal for comfort from a loved one and is the path to healing.

On the book cover, Phillip R. Shaver, Ph.D., University of California is quoted as saying, "this book puts psychological, developmental, physiological, and cultural influences on crying (and not crying) into a single framework, making sense of a deeply human experience that often seems beyond words." Alan Schore (Emotional Self-Regulation guru) also endorses Nelson's work.

For me, this excellent read reinforced crying as an attachment behaviour across the lifespan. It is designed to protect survival in infancy and it is a powerful determinant of social connection throughout life.

The Need for Safety
(An e-mail exchange with the mother of a five-year old boy)

Hi Susan

I don't know if you do this but I need some advice tonight. I don't know if you have time to talk on the phone or can just charge me for an e-mail session. I don't know. We move tomorrow and Anthony is really angry. He's been doing really well and excited to go to the new house but I have no idea how to help him. A friend of his came to say goodbye to him and he smashed a gate door in her face. We are invited to go to a neighbour's house for dinner and he won't go. I sat with him and tried to help him feel the emotions and he kicked me and spit at me over and over. He doesn't want to say goodbye to anyone and he doesn't want me with him he won't let me hold him no matter what I say. We've had a really good couple of days and I really want to help him but I have no idea how. Any thoughts would be appreciated.

Marjorie

Dear Marjorie

Poor little Anthony, he is not feeling emotionally safe right now and his primitive brain has taken over. He feels like there is a predator at the door and he has moved into defending himself. His spitting and kicking are instinctual much like a cat hissing to try to get something to get out of the way. This is attacking energy because he is in transition and it is too much to bear.

Anthony is not angry, he is frustrated. There is nothing he can do to change his situation and the only place for him to go is to his tears so that he can adapt. I encourage you to stay with him and when he is out of his fight/flight instinct (outside the incident), calmly in a soothing voice say "I know on the one hand you want to stay in this house and on the other you are both excited and afraid about where we are going to live". "I will keep you safe, you can count on me and we will all be together as a family". Good-byes are so tough on little people and just going to someone else's house for dinner is too much with all the chatter of what tomorrow will bring and how much you will be missed by your neighbours. Focus on the next time you will see them. Come up with a plan that keeps Anthony out of the confusion tomorrow so that he can just be put in the car and taken to his new home. Ideally, his new room could be set up just like his old room before he gets there. Do you have someone to help you with the children and the unpacking? Is there somewhere he can go that isn't confusing and busy, busy with chaos?

You could talk about the invisible string that holds the whole family together in the old house and how it will be present in the new house. Let him know that you know this is so hard for him and that his good mind will help him to get through it with courage. If he is into Batman or Spiderman make him a cape out of a towel to protect him and help him to feel safe as he uses his courage to take this big leap.

Most of all, you stay calm, keep the surroundings calm and provide him with the attachment objects that he needs to hold on to until he lands in a safe place. Hopefully, he has helped to pack some of his belongings that he can unpack when he is in his new home. The content of the boxes will feel like presents to him.

He may need to rage to get all of the cortisol and adrenaline out of his body. Sit by him and coach him to get it out. He will start to cry and the chemistry will change. Even if he won't let you in his room. Stay outside his door and tell him you will keep him safe.

Try to keep things as peaceful as possible for this evening with as few people as possible saying good-bye.

Hope this helps. Any further questions, I am near a computer and can respond for the next 20 min. I don't have phone availability right now but I do after 10:30 tomorrow morning.

Hold on tight - you will get through this bumpy patch.

Warmly,

Susan

Hi Susan

Thank you so much for your prompt reply it helped us so much tonight. I had no idea what to do. I stayed calm the whole time before I emailed you but it seemed there was just no getting through to him. He wouldn't let me in his room so I gave him some space but then I got your email and I went up to him and he was asleep. He woke up at 8:30 and I went into him and gently talked to him and cuddled with him 'cause he was calm. I told him I know how hard this is and that he's safe and I'm right here to help him, etc... He wanted to read some books on his rocking chair with me which he hasn't asked to do in a long time so we did. Then I tucked him back into bed and said I know it's hard to say goodbye, don't feel bad that you couldn't say goodbye to everybody tonight and then the tears flowed. He cried in my arms saying he will never get to say goodbye and see them again. He calmed after I told him I promised we would see them again and we have already arranged for our neighbours to come see our new place and he can show them his new park and he was happy about that. I have a day planned for me and the kids tomorrow so we won't be around for any of the chaos

Thanks, Susan

I will be in touch about next meeting time.

Why Do We Cry?

Normally, there is a continuous flow of tears across the exposed area of the eyes. This is primarily a means of cleansing and lubricating the eyes. When we cry, there is literally a flood of tears, more than the duct-work can handle. These tears are stimulated by two things: irritation and emotion. As far as we know human beings are the only species which cries because of its emotions – both positive and negative.

We cry because of sadness or grief and we cry because of joy and extreme pleasure. The key to why we cry, whether because of positive or negative feelings is a little structure in the middle of the brain called the amygdala. The amygdala is sometimes referred to as the "smoke-alarm" of the brain since it is always on the lookout for danger; but it also responds to those events which are unexpectedly positive – like winning the lottery.

When the amygdala senses an extreme condition it sends a signal to a big bundle of nerves call the trigeminal nerve which controls all of our face and jaw. Part of this bundle is the lachrymal nerve which stimulate the lachrymal glands. So, the amygdala fires, the impulse travels to the lachrymal gland and we cry.

What's a "good cry"? When we cry because we are sad, a chemical called manganese is flushed out of the body along with many other stress hormones. Removing these hormones can elevate our mood. (There are enough toxins in our tears that if they are collected and injected into a small rodent the animal will be killed!)

When the body is under constant stress fluid is diverted away from the eyes and the result is a dry-eyed condition.

Family Relations

"Giving and receiving emotional intimacy or love must feel safe before loving can happen."

Alarm

This is my day to cry the tears I have held for fourteen days. Two weeks ago today, at the end of a delightful family Thanksgiving celebration, my mother, my anchor, fell over the corner of the open dishwasher door as she was helping to clear the dinner table. The world stopped for a moment. I fell to her side and wrapped her in my arms and held her close as she, in her words, tried to compose herself. I instinctively knew this was the dreaded moment that life would catch-up to her eighty-two years and that I needed to become the dominant person in our hierarchy. I carefully ran my fingers down her left hip. Feeling the bone fractured just under her skin, while continuing to hold her in her fear, I started giving soft but crisp instructions to my daughter and husband: pillows and blankets to cushion her on the floor; a wet cloth for her bleeding hand; a lubricant to remove her rings; a 911 call for an ambulance with instructions that there be no sirens and that the paramedics be as discreet as possible. My son-in-law with both his bigness and gentleness led my grandchildren downstairs to the playroom. My grand-daughter was crying for her "Great".

Within ten minutes, two paramedics were standing in my kitchen and then lifting with ease my little mother onto the stretcher, asking me to follow the ambulance in the car. Determined not to show any expression on my face, I assured the driver that it would be better for everyone if I were to ride in the cab of the ambulance. The ride was swift with no sirens. The triage nurse in the emergency department at the hospital was clearly at her stress threshold for the day, no eye contact, abrupt questions and little time to wait for the answers. Stepping in quickly, I did my best to bridge the gap that was dividing the space she left between my mother and the journey mom was about to begin. X-rays, blood tests, heart monitors, more medical history questions flooded the next three hours.

My mother remained pleasant and appreciative of the professionals who were making decisions about her care, while she hung onto my hand for reassurance. A few minutes before midnight, she was wheeled away from me. Our eyes met and we smiled. "See you in a couple of hours", I promised. I now realize that I lost all sense of tiredness, hunger and even toileting. All my attention was to get care for my mother. My brain was busily numbing out and tuning out anything that was getting in the way of me doing my job. My job is the work of attachment. I am destined to take care of those whom for I am responsible – it is my primary work. My vulnerability was defended. I did lose my feelings. There is nothing wrong with my brain. This is no mistake, my brain did what it is supposed to do so that I could attend to the woman I most love and to whom I am attached. I now understand how defendedness can get stuck. As a baby coming into this world , my neural circuitry for pain was calibrated optimally through the birthing process. Those people who had difficult entries into the world, have their defenses evoked by their sensitivities or their woundedness and have no way out of the maze of futility. I was fortunate both for my organic birth and for a mother who shielded me from my vulnerabilities. I knew that in time my defenses would come down and reverse themselves.

My husband, David, sat with me stoically in the empty surgical waiting room. Each minute seemed interminable. The surgeon was to give us a report before Mom went to the recovery room. After two hours of waiting, thinking the worst, we found a nurse who checked on the outcome of surgery and learned my mother was on her way to her room on the surgical floor, having finished the necessary time in recovery. The surgeon was too tired to talk with us. David went home and I found my way to Mom's room.

For the next several days, I continued to feel neither hunger nor fatigue. I carried on with my work schedule, with my consultation with Gordon and with my role as oldest daughter. I was at the hospital by 8:00 a.m., stayed until 3:00 or 4:00 p.m., headed to work until 9:00 p.m. and then a check-in back at the hospital. Mom's nurses were different each shift and I wanted to be the match-maker so that the baton of attachment was passed from caregiver to caregiver. She moved between critical care and surgery for almost two weeks. I watched with wonder as Mom adjusted to each piece of new and bad news about her heart. Her hip was improving like a younger woman's but her heart rate couldn't find a stable rhythm. She was in atrial fibrillation, with sustained heart rates as high as 160 bpm. Mom was confident that the doctors would find the right medication to stabilize her and she would be going "somewhere" soon. In fact, she told me that on one of the medications, she had experienced a very pleasant floating away sensation, much like she anticipated death might resemble. Soon after this disclosure, in my numbness, I was able to stand by her side, hold her hand and watch as she was given an intravenous medication (by a very young internist) to shock her heart into a normal rhythm. Her face contorted, her body writhed, she gasped for air and then relaxed into a regular heart rate for two minutes. It was at this place of stillness, that I realized that I must insist a heart specialist get involved. An older internist agreed that the current treatment was futile. I finally felt my tears.

An angel of mercy, an alpha cardiologist with an interest in atrial fibrillation, stepped in, reviewed the file and swept into my Mom's critical care unit announcing that he could help solve her problem with the medication he was about to prescribe. It worked. Three days later, she was discharged from the hospital in my care. Instead of taking her back to a convalescent home in her hometown, Mom suggested she stay near us for a month in a Retirement Home, which provides rehabilitation services and personal care. In her words, her "community of healing energy (attachment)" was right here in Guelph and among all of us she would recover more swiftly and with joy.

Today, fourteen days after the accident, I can see that all the help my Mom needs to recover is in place, I finally feel my parasympathetic nervous system slowing down. I also feel the backlash. I cry an ocean of tears. I am truly empty. The defenses in my sympathetic nervous system lower. Once again, I am reminded that life is fragile. I am incredibly hungry. I am freezing cold. My tiredness is overwhelming. My alarm system is on hold for now.

I will be her shield from too much separation. I will protect her sensitivities, her wounds, and her dignity. I accept the alpha position for now – until she takes it back, which won't be long. I love her.

Christmas Cake and the Womb of Attachment

Today, my daughter, my five year old grand-daughter and I traveled to my mother's home to bake the traditional Christmas cake. Four generations of Dafoe women in the kitchen were clearly in hierarchical positions, much like Marushka dolls with the great-grandmother ("Great") on the outside and the next three generations fitting inside in order of age. For many generations this ritual has not changed.

The great-grand-mother is always in charge of giving instructions in generational sequence. As the grand-mother it is my responsibility to first purchase all of the ingredients and then measure each and place in appointed bowls; as the mother, my daughter is to cut up all of the fruit except the pineapple and this year, the great- grandmother decided that her great grand-daughter was old enough to cut it up with a semi-sharp knife. As I, the grand-mother, measure somewhat carefully, "Great" is supervising the entire process making suggestions to each of us. She was unhappy with the texture of the butter, after insisting that I leave it out overnight to gently soften it for smooth mixing. It is a cold day today and the butter got hard in the trunk of the car *en route*. After much problem solving using "on the one hand we could do this and the other hand we could do that", the great-grand-mother led us to a plural oneness. Her reset button engaged and she agreed that the microwave on defrost would bring the butter to exactly the correct consistency.

The mixing of the ingredients has historical significance within our family. As the grand-mother, my responsibility is to dredge the cut-up fruit with flour before the mixing of the wet and dry ingredients. The eldest ("Great") starts the process and then passes the wooden spoon (baton) to the youngest (my grand-daughter) who passes the spoon to her mother, who then finally passes it back to her mother (me). As the next in line to the alpha position, I must prove myself worthy of taking charge one day. I mix and mix and mix under the watchful eye of my mother. She decided when I was to pour the mixture into the pan. It is always the oldest woman who then opens the oven door and sets the timer.

While this year's Christmas cake is baking we decide to enjoy lunch together. During lunch, my grand-daughter wanted us to change places in every combination possible. The oldest and the youngest were invited to sit together on one side of the table while the two middle people sat on the other side. Then we were arranged in a grand-mother and grand-daughter formation, followed by a mother and a daughter. We finished our meal sitting around the table with "Great" sitting at the head, Grandma (me) sitting next to her, my daughter next and finally my grand-daughter. We completed the circle (square) from the oldest through to the youngest generation. My grand-daughter figured out her position by understanding all the combinations of the women who have gone before her. She knows her rightful place inside the womb of attachment as does her mother, her grand-mother and her great-grand-mother.

May you re-enter your womb of attachment and feel the safety of acceptance during the holidays.

Marriage and Attachment
(An e-mail discussion with a colleague)

I've been thinking about your post since about five minutes after you left it on the forum. You have provided all of us with an excellent overview of Emotionally Focused Therapy (EFT) and I'm impressed with your examples of how Gordon's paradigm provides a template for Sue Gordon's work. I, too, love the interplay of mapping one model on another.

Your first example of a mature marriage being egalitarian including that oscillating balance of moving to take care of the other when a need is noticed is also found in Dr.Boszormenyi-Nagy's Contextual Therapy. Nagy based many of the dimensions of his model on the work of Martin Buber (*I and Thou*). Gail Palmer in Ottawa, who is a Sue Johnson's protégé, spoke about Buber's influence on EFT in an address she gave at a conference at the University of Guelph in 2003. Gordon often quotes Buber. I am thinking that I would love to hear a philosophical discussion among all of these Masters.

Your second example from one of Gordon's examples in a Power to Parent DVD (the hypothetical marriage proposal) where the one says to the other, "don't expect me to do anything for you that you could do for yourself"

captures in a nutshell the thinking of not only many of the couples with whom I have worked in Ontario but also their parenting styles. One of the private nursery schools here in town encourages parents never to do for a child what a child can do for him/herself. The bottom line is that partnering and parenting are, of course, both influencing and impeding the other. Some of the family systems thinking has steered us into this confusion surrounding "enmeshment", "co-dependence" and "differentiation". Buber, Nagy, Neufeld and Johnson have it figured out that we need to stand beside one another in love (to be both separate from and a part of each other).

Sue Johnson's model which provides leadership in healing "attachment breaks" comes with such compassion, generosity of spirit and empathy, I can sometimes hear Gordon's voice in unison with Sue's.

Yes Todd, I think there is a place for EFT in couples' work. At the same time, I must confess that as I transition my practice from marriage and family work to parent consulting, I am noticing that couples seem to be working through their own stuff by keeping the focus on developing new eyes for their kids. Those new eyes seem to generalize right into the couple relationship. I have not had to repair one attachment break in six month. To my own astonishment - peppered in delight - couples are noticing each other's sensitivities, vulnerabilities and defendedness and the impact of shaming, blaming and withdrawal. I am witnessing parents who are committed to being the best bet for their kids becoming the best bet for one another. On the one hand, I know that it is Gordon's paradigm which has had the biggest impact in my life and on the other hand the work of the other great masters like Buber, Rogers, Perls, Bowlby, and Johnson have given me substance so that I can connect my own dots from time to time. (The 4-yr old in me says, "I can do it myself"!)

I would also like to say that Les Greenberg's work on Client-Centered Therapy is important to my dot-connecting. Emotional experience and regulation for the client and empathy, respect and genuineness on the part of the therapist pull together a powerful model which influences change and adaptation.

Thanks for this opportunity to "chat" with you.

Soft-hearted Chanukamas

This year with the economy taking a swipe at my family, we have decided that instead of a huge hoard of commercially produced presents in our Chanukamus stockings, we would bridge the change with meaningful songs, poems, riddles and philosophic statements which would fill our ears and our hearts.

In Christianity, the true gift of Christmas is the redemption of the world through the birth of a child who embodies love, faithfulness, humility and promise. Jewish families come together in November-December of each year to celebrate the holiday of Chanukah (which means dedication) to recall a momentous event – an uprising in the name of religious freedom. According to the ancient legend, after the uprising occurred and it was time to rededicate the Temple, holy oil was needed to light the Temple's great menorah for eight days. Miraculously, the only small vessel of holy oil to be found burned for the required eight days.

In our home, in order to honour both traditions, we light the menorah which signifies truth, light and life and we have in the past given gifts to demonstrate our love. This year we will continue to light the menorah and extend the hope and peace of Christmas beyond the day by replacing gifts with words which are really our actions and intentions.

This new way of doing things came easily to my five year old grand-daughter. This year, her roots of attachment have grown into experiencing the purity of love for the first time. She came up with an idea that we could make hearts for everyone by melting down her old crayons and shaping them into a heart mold. We scoured the craft cupboard and found an old heart-shaped soap mold which fit her vision. Alas, the crayons didn't work! After some tears, we did discover that the crayons could colour melted candle wax. After pouring the wax into the mold, she muscularly sprinkled golden glitter on each heart and waited patiently until they set. This sequence in the process was repeated many times in order to accumulate fourteen hearts. "Look Grand-ma", she said as she carefully released the thirteenth heart from its form, "we have a whole bunch of *soft hearts* to give to everyone in the family so that our invisible strings will stay connected". Earlier that day, we had taken turns reading from one of her favourite books, "Invisible Strings".

Truth, light, love, faithfulness, humility and promise came from her in one statement. I have a sense that we will be dedicating this holiday season to a

new tradition. Symbolism will rekindle
the warmth of our dual tradition and
inside this shield, we will share our
fears, our hopes and our dreams for
the future.

The Sound of her Voice

In a recent study at the University of Wisconsin, three groups of young girls performed anxiety-producing tasks (public speaking and math problems). On completion, girls in one of the groups had 15 minutes of contact with their mothers (which could include a hug or kiss); those in the second group received a telephone call from their mother, and members of the third group watched a neutral film and had no parental contact.

Stress (measured by amount of *cortisol*) increased in all three groups as a result of the tasks. At the end of an hour after the tasks the cortisol levels of girls in both of the groups which had contact with their mothers had declined (*and there was no difference in whether the contact was physical or by 'phone*). Further, in both of these "contact" groups the levels of *oxytocin* – a hormone strongly linked to emotional bonding –increased within 15 minutes and the effects lasted for an hour!

The authors of the story are wondering if text messaging would also have the same effect and whether the effect would be true for boys. More research is planned.

Moral of the story: if you can't hold on to your kids physically try for verbal connection.

(It would be interesting to know whether what the mothers said, or how they said it had differential effects. That is, were there some interactions that had even greater effects on lowering cortisol and/or on raising oxytocin.)

The link to this article was original posted on the Neufeld Campus to which one of her colleagues responded:

Interesting … one of the 'strategies' that we have been putting in place in schools to support kids who are highly alarmed is to have them chat with their moms over the phone. With much controversy, of course, in our behaviourist environments! We have found it incredibly successful. You can feel the calm return to the child as you hear his
(her) voice move in the conversation.

I have also made this part of our summer camp strategies. If we have a home-sick child, we schedule a time to talk to mom just before bedtime. Amazing how this works (again, controversial because the common belief is that phoning mom will just escalate the homesickness). Last year we had a little guy who got a 'phone call from his mom every evening (notice the invitation rather than waiting for him to ask). The cabin leader (who was a dad himself and very intuitive about what kids needed) would walk with him to the office, get the call and then put the boy on the phone. If he started to miss mom, he would talk to him about what he could tell mom about his day when she called that night .

What Happened to that Loving Feeling?

Looking at married love or emotional intimacy through the eyes of attachment begins with our own childhood. Emotional intimacy is that warm feeling of closeness that is vital for a growing child. Expressing love happens at about age four or five when the child gives his/her heart to the parent and trusts that the parent will hold it carefully without tampering with its fragility.

Giving and receiving emotional intimacy or love must feel safe before loving can happen. We can truly love if we are aware of our own wounds. If we are closed off from our wounds, it is almost impossible to love the wounds in another.

Both physically beautiful, my clients Sandra and Ken, are a couple who find loving confusing and impossible. Their love is buried and has grown cold under their anger, anxiety, alarm and resentment. Their past wounds are too much to bear. By not addressing their childhood woundedness, both are sitting in a stagnant pool of emotion that needs to be expressed. Sandra demands love but it is too much work for Ken. When he takes loving actions as she requests, she is unsatisfied feels unfulfilled and he is frustrated.

Authentic love is given spontaneously and with warmth, it feels like a surprise gift. Ken has no desire to give love because he has never truly received it and refuses to grieve what he did not have as a child. Sandra believes Ken doesn't want to be present with her and help her with the household and parenting chores. When he offers help, she rejects him. Ken cannot find a way to feel significant.

Ken and Sandra fell into love by projecting onto each other what they thought would be pleasure-producing. They each fell in love with the belief that they were being loved. However, neither can accept in the other the imperfections nor the attributes which they are blinded to in themselves. Cut off from their own emotions, they tricked themselves into believing they mattered and belonged to each other. This has not sustained their marriage.

As their match-maker, my work is to restore their attachment to each other. Both are searching for the healing balm of being cared for by the other. Both are capable of satiating the hunger in the other. Finding a place in which each feels safe to give his/her heart to the other will ultimately bring them to a place where they can begin to grow deeper roots both together and separately. On the one hand, their love may rebound. On the other hand,

there may not be the space nor the
springboard to do so.

Issues

"Adults refer themselves to a professional for help with anxiety. However, children are referred for behavioural problems."

Age is More

Age is more than the sum of its parts. Age isn't simply a matter of the number of days, years or decades lived and it is more than the collection of experiences which one has between birth and the present.

If age were simply defined as a collection of events, however meaningful or playful, however painful or life changing then age would be simply be a matter of storage – a matter of listing on the calendar all of the days of one's life and marking on them whatever happened. Age would be no more than the catalogue of one's life – subject to revision and to new editions as memory and mind changed over time.

And age is more than the body in which we currently reside. Our physical being, with all of its warts and blemishes, all of its grinding and stiffness is still – in a sense - who we were and yet we are different with almost every one of our cells having been replaced many times over with the passage of time. Age is more than sensory capacity; more than cognitive ability; more than physical agility. Age is all of these but it is still more. What marks our age as unique is the life lived with others. Everyone has roughly the same experiences and milestones; everyone has roughly the same trajectory of bodily development and in the end decay. What marks our true age is the collection of encounters which we have had with others: teachers in grade school; sweethearts; team-mates; family members; children; colleagues and caregivers. As well, there are the money lenders; the vendors of our homes and houses and (if we are fortunate) our investment advisors. Age is more than predictability; it is embracing randomness.

Age as it's experienced when one is alone, is the movie one is able to play in one's head. For some there is only one, solitary actor on the screen of one's mind; for others there are two or three meaningful leading actors with perhaps a small supporting cast, and for others there is a mob scene of extras, swirling about with no apparent purpose other than to fill the stage and the time to watch them.

Age is more than years lived; it is more than accomplishments or failures; it is more than good health or otherwise. Age is the experience of being a social being; it is the true attachments to others and them to us. Age is being able to sit with oneself, knowing that we matter (or have mattered) to others. Measured in this way the very old can still be very young and alive. But age is more than chasing youth; it is reconciling the past and accepting the future.

Eating and Attachment

Nature did not intend either eating or feeding to be a stressful experience in anyone's life, especially for the overburdened parents of young children. Cajoling children into a lifetime of healthy eating has back-fired. Our children are developing disordered eating. Where have we gone awry?

Feeding should be an act of generosity, with no strings nor expectations attached. Eating should be with the people who shield us from the expectations of the world, with those who love us unconditionally and with those who understand that pressure creates resistance. Every child possesses the instinct to do the opposite of what is expected and to withhold cooperation. This is neither inherited nor learned. It is totally dependent on the context of the child's relationship with responsible adults.

Children who turn away from their food often sense the pressure of the will of others. All children are allergic to coercion and sniff it out at a very early age. Coaxing a child to eat using either threats or rewards sets up the child's wish to be in charge. Asking your child what she would like to eat, which chair she would like to sit in and when a good time to eat would be, puts the child in the dominant position to make decisions which parents are ordained to make. Giving your child this power puts her in the position to refuse or misuse her food. Parents are in charge of the decision-making about what to eat (choosing of course something you know your child will love), when to eat and where to sit. The dinner table is no place for democracy!

Since physical hunger is natural, eating should be the natural response to food which is generously given. If the child feels, "I must eat what is in front of me", he will balk. Take the pressure off. Remove the expectations around "having to eat". Provide the food with no comment, depersonalize any rejections, and work on the relationship with your child using all of your warmth. Delight in their very being. Never give praise, because that suggests to the child that he must eat to please mommy or daddy instead of for the sheer desire to be involved in the eating ritual. When your child does eat, hold onto your comments. Remember: eating is as natural as sleeping. Neither requires encouragement or comment on your part. All that is required is a table, a chair for each family member and food that is prepared with love, joy and generosity.

Studies have shown that children who are full of stress hormones (which also inhibit growth) do not sense their own hunger. For children small enough, I would encourage holding that child lovingly on your lap and feeding him while you eat. This act of attachment lowers the stress in the child's body and improves digestion.

Overeaters are unaware of their body's signals that let them know they are full. Reducing chaos by turning outside stimulation off, decreasing pressure to eat and increasing the warmth of connections within the family will help the child to tune into his body's natural rhythm. Eating and attachment are inextricably linked.

Emotional Regulation

The problem with emotional regulation in preschoolers is huge. Currently, the Ontario public school system is rating a child's ability to emotionally regulate without taking into account the reality of how emotions behave. Emotions are meant to be moving, increasing and decreasing in intensity in response to our world. They are meant to affect us. Emotions inform us about our surroundings. The experience and expression of emotions is vital to our emotional and mental health. During a typical day, we should experience a wide range of emotions in a wide range of intensities.

It seems the idea of "regulation" is that we should not be affected strongly by our emotions - that our emotions should not move us. And yet they are designed to move us to action in response to our environment. A child who is dysregulated is a child who is experiencing a strong emotion. True, a regulated child does make OUR lives easier, but it is in no way helpful, healthy or good for the child. Experiencing each of their emotions individually,

clearly, and in a variety of intensities develops an emotional language necessary for healthy growth and emotional consciousness. *(Pamela Whyte, Neufeld Virtual Campus, November 2012)*

Dr. Gordon Neufeld, a Vancouver Developmental Psychologist points out that as a society, we need to replace the idea of "regulation" with both the understanding of mixed feelings and the adaptive process. Neuroscience indicates that after the pre-frontal cortex has some time to develop, the child will be able to hold back their immediate reactions to feelings. In other words, children will be able to experience their feelings without having to act on them or to act them out. They will be able to hold on to their feelings until they find a safe place (the arms of a loving parent) where the depths of their emotion can be experienced, as opposed to spilling out their feelings in contexts where the feelings can be misunderstood. Asking a child not to act out their feelings BEFORE they get to the natural state where their frontal cortex is well enough developed to put him/her in control, can only cause attachment issues, emotional numbing, alarm and problems of identification (identifying oneself as "I am an aggressive child", "I am a bad child", "I am a dysregulated child", etc.). *(Pamela Whyte, Neufeld Virtual Campus, November, 2012)*

Our job is to lovingly support the child through the adaptive process, a developmental stage in the maturation process. It is during this time when children realize they can make mistakes, benefit from failure and become prepared to navigate the path of life. Until adaptation unfolds in development, it is up to responsible adults to move things out of the way to make the world more bearable for the children in their care.

We cannot expect to live in our world without being strongly moved. If we strive to numb our feelings with drugs, push down our strong feelings or to "think" them away, we are likely to slip into depression or generalized anxiety. If our emotions are denied, they become transformed but they may leak out in other ways that are more socially acceptable. In a world where the human condition has become medicalized, a diagnosis has credibility, emotions don't! Giving room, inviting emotions and providing a safe place to cry can transform what appears to be an insurmountable state of intense anxiety, frustration or aggression into tears of futility, a point at which we realize that something cannot or will not work. This is a vital part of the adaptation process. Regulation naturally happens through this adaptation process and it's where we develop a sense of courage, empowerment and resilience.

Letter to a TV Parent Consultant

With interest, I have watched your "Parenting Show" on Rogers Cable TV for the past several Sunday mornings. Overall, I have great concerns about your advice. In particular, this week's show about sleep was most alarming.

Babies have only two ways to communicate to us and that is through their smiles and their tears. To only invite smiles and cooperation is to disinvite tears which are expressions of their need for us. I have visions of a two-year old standing at a gate in his bedroom crying to be heard, to be invited into the safety of loving arms, to be reassured that there is room for whatever they are experiencing. It is a sad vision! The picture of an older child standing at his parent's bedroom door with a lock to keep him out of their space is just as sad.

I am not certain if you have read any of Alan Schore's work about emotional self-regulation. In essence, Dr. Schore, who is a highly respected neuroscientist, is telling us that it is up to the responsible adults in a child's life to do the emotional regulating until a child is developed enough to do it for him/herself. By expecting that children can take of themselves before they are ready we are actually increasing the likelihood that they will remain dependent on the adults longer. In fact, science is telling us that adolescence is prolonged and maturity is impeded. I invite you to review the literature on the changes now being seen (via MRI's) in the current teenage brain research.

It is a disservice to parents and their growing children for you to suggest that training or teaching a child how and when to sleep is possible. Children develop as the wiring in their brains makes connections. It is up to the parents to shield children from expectations outside their competency and not to traumatize them thereby prolonging their maturation.

We cannot sculpt children but we can provide conditions that will help them to grow up.

Divorce and Children - Damage Control in Times of Detaching

Inside the adversarial culture of divorce, children of a marriage often become pawns in emotional crossfire. Even when intentions are honourable, in their differences and conflicts, in their endless inherent imperfections, divorcing couples are blinded by the competitive dynamics between the self and the whole. When one person wants to "win" at any cost, the outcome for the children can be damaging.

In good times, love, support and nurturing given unconditionally inside a safe emotional relationship is what most parents strive for, until divorce demands detaching from the other parent. Most often and unintentionally, the parents may lose sight of the importance of children having an invitation to exist in the presence of each other.

Children whose parents are divorced have the capacity to be "just kids", if the parents are willing to see them through a developmental lens. For children, neuro-development is dependent on having "rest" in relationships. Rest is a place or condition in which children do not feel driven; driven to please, to take sides, to succeed, to take part in, or to

interact. Feeling shielded and safe inside this place where there are no expectations and no urge to please or to take care of the wounds of their parents, children's brains make connections in their neural wiring as maturation unfolds.

When children are put in the position of taking the side of one parent or the other, or of hearing any negative information from one parent about the other, it typically takes a lifetime to overcome the effects. It is not uncommon, for one parent who is needing validation to insist that the children of the marriage read the accusations outlined in the divorce papers! No one, especially a vulnerable child, can see themself as separate from either parent. Any accusation against one parent is an accusation against a child. When children become preoccupied with making decisions about what to do and where they fit, they develop a sense that they are in some way responsible for the marital breakdown and that they are now responsible to fill their own needs. Understandably, this creates anxiety and alarm.

On the other hand, children with divorcing parents can often adapt well when each parent strives to keep them loyal to the other. Managing the stress of a divorce is up to the adults. Parents who do a good job at managing the stress and who remain focussed on the needs of their offspring are often surprised at how well they do adjust. When parents are sensitive to the innate need for children to be loyal to both and invest in keeping the invisible ties active, their children's resilience can grow.

Parents who are divorcing have the power to promote the continued healthy development of their children when they can work together to keep the relationship roots with each other nourished and flourishing. Divorce damage control for children is essential - now and always. To redeem the future, we must restore emotional security for kids who get caught in the tyranny of detaching parents. The marriage might be over - but parenting continues.

Ritalin Gone Wrong

Re: "Ritalin Gone Wrong", The *National Post*, Jan. 31, 2012

Before summarizing this article by Prof. Emeritus Sroufe of the University of Minnesota's Institute of Child Development it's probably a good idea to present the two opposing views published in letters to the editor:
Dr. Carl A. Rubino, (Psychologist) in Perth, Ontario writes, "I have never encountered a published article that says, "studies show (drugs) work for four to eight weeks".
Dr. Murray S. Katz, (Physician) in Montreal states "of all the medications developed in child psychiatry in the past 30 years, Ritalin remains one of the most effective and safest." He also argues ADHD is largely an inherited disorder...a physical problem of the brain (and that) many of these children have learning disorders as well as psychiatric co-morbidities and these do require additional interventions to medication."

(The jury is still out, but here's Sroufe's position:)
In the last 30 years there has been a 20-fold increase in the consumption of drugs for attention deficit disorder. In almost every short-term study there is an improvement in the child's behaviour and, while these drugs do increase the ability to focus when they are given to children over long periods of time they neither improve school achievement, nor reduce behaviour problems, and the drugs can have serious side effects, including stunting growth.

Ritalin is a stimulant. So why does it appear to calm children down? Actually, all children (whether diagnosed with ADD or not) respond to stimulants in the same way: increased ability to concentrate (in class, for example) especially on boring tasks but there is no improvement in broader learning abilities. And this improved ability to focus disappears because their brains learn to tolerate the drug. When parents take their children off the drug, behaviour worsens because the child's body has adapted to the drug and what is seen is a withdrawal effect.

In research on parenting practices, genetic and environmental factors, it was found that it was the environment that best predicted development of ADD. Neurological anomalies at birth, IQ and infant temperament and activity level did not predict ADD. Giving drugs to children is an attempt to get everyone off the hook for creating better child rearing practices – everyone except the children.
If drugs, which studies show work for four to eight weeks, are not the answer, what is? Many of these children have

anxiety or depression, others are showing family stresses. We need to treat them as individuals.

To which I would add, they lack the safety and nourishment which attachment to caring parents could provide.

Under the Diagnosis: Anxiety, Agitation and Panic

Have you ever wondered as an adult what you have in common with a child? In today's society, the pressures of parents, teachers, care-givers and children have reached unprecedented high levels. All are experiencing the powerful chemicals produced in the brain and body that make us feel awful. All are at high risk of being diagnosed with depression, anxiety, panic disorders, phobias, attention-deficit disorders, hyperactivity disorders, even relationship difficulties.

If as children, we repeatedly feel fear and rage – for instance, from a parenting/teaching/care-giving style that regularly involves shouting, demands and commands, criticism and angry facial expressions, the brain does what it is supposed to do: it alarms the child. In the alarm state, part of the brain is moving the child to caution and part of the brain is defending the child's fragility against the alarm. This kind of competition in the brain generates a number of diagnoses. Under the diagnosis lies a hormonal hell. The release of feel good hormones (opioids and oxytocin) is blocked so feeling calm is out of the question. Not being relieved by the comfort and warm physical presence of a responsible adult, the child can

become accustomed to the high levels of chemicals (cortisol, epinephrine and norepinephrine) which are being pumped out of the adrenal glands in times of stress. In fact, high levels of cortisol make us feel anxious, angry and irritable and even colour our thoughts, feelings, and perceptions with a sense of threat. Then everything we need to do is far too hard and we are trapped into a constant state of hyperarousal. In this state, we are likely to cope by having the impulse to fight or to withdraw and avoid life. There is more. The brain's chemicals, such as endorphins and dopamine which regulate things like emotion, pain, pleasure and motivation are disrupted. The bottom line is that the child is stuck in development.

For recovery, the body cannot be injected with the feel good twins, oxytocin and opioids. The only way to activate these chemicals in the brain is through warm human connection. Basically providing what didn't happen in infancy and early childhood. Adults refer themselves to a professional for help with anxiety. However, children are referred for behavioural problems. There is no quick way to turn off the chemistry of alarm but by replicating a nurturing environment and cultivating functional relationships, alarm can be progressively turned down and eventually off.

Unfortunately, the prevailing practice in both parenting and teaching is more focused on managing behaviour than in cultivating relationships. When we can look into and under the diagnosis, it makes sense that the healing power is within us. When we feel we really matter to those who surround us we give our high-jacked brain a second chance.

Journal Entries

"I was feeling the void of not being chosen to lead the County away from what I saw as obvious blindness"

Digital Divide

Oh, how I love my technology! I can do the banking sitting at the kitchen table, FaceTime my grandchildren in Newfoundland and London, make "time-together" arrangements with my Guelph grandchildren, receive my mother's crisp messages, schedule appointments for my office, locate YouTube videos to help me learn how to play the ukulele and stay in touch with the big world. However, there is a dark side.

Sherry Turkle, after fifteen years of studying our lives in the digital world discusses how "technology has become the architect of our intimacies" (*Alone Together*,2011). In our pursuit of closeness, we have looked to technology for ways to be in relationship by gathering thousands of Twitter and Facebook friends and "confusing tweets and wall posts with authentic communication" and genuine intimacy.

University of Chicago social neuroscientist, John T. Cacioppo, the world's leading expert on loneliness, argues that we have everything to gain and everything to lose by how well we manage or don't manage our need for social and familial bonds. His research has shown that the greater the frequency of online interaction, the greater the loneliness.

Clearly, the unbridled use of technology can be detrimental to family life and child development. When I was a child there were rules around the use of the telephone. There was nothing that would upset my father more than being interrupted during dinner with the disturbing ring of our black dial phone, which was plugged into the kitchen wall. He would huff and puff at us as if it were our fault that our friends were so thoughtless. For me, I thought that the source of the problem was more because of my father's deafness.

Independently and quietly, I justified his reaction as more likely to be the sound of the ringing amplified by his chest-bearing hearing aid which I thought probably produced some kind of echoing that created a "mind-blowing" frequency. After 50 years of not thinking about his facial contortions, snorts and *gutterances*, I understand that he was protecting our family time. In fact, the limits he imposed around the use of the telephone are now worth considering as we think about the impact of a powerful digital world on family life. How do we create the conditions so our children can both reach their full potential as individuals and also get along in a society that demands arms-length involvement with others on Facebook, Twitter and Instant Messaging? One parent I talked with says that time on his digital devices not only keeps him connected to work, but to his identity as a person. His phone, in particular, allows him: to look at websites that feed his curiosities; to see who is following him on Twitter; to remain connected to his friends and to keep being himself without having to give up everything in order to be a parent. This is the parent of an adolescent son who wonders why he can't have access to screens - whenever he wants to - like his father does. This is an adolescent son who yearns for live human connectedness and times to hike in nature with his family and knows that screen time does not fill him up like his parents could.

Children are "hungry for uninterrupted parent time, especially in a culture that has come to place children at the centre of their lives" (Dr. Steiner-Adair, *National Post*, Sept 21, 2013). So, pushing a swing in the park, attending a child's soccer game, or sitting at Grandma's kitchen table all while checking Facebook, email or text messages while being involved in a Twitter debate at the same time divides attention and those who need relationship most are suffering. No justification would convince my now dearly departed father that this is O.K.

Screens spoil the appetite for what we really need. When we displace healthy adult connections, we are denying ourselves and especially our children the essential need for fulfilling human interaction. This leads me to wonder if the new developmental stage of "the never-grow-ups" is the result of being starved by the essentially empty elements of technology. Dr. Gordon Neufeld, in his revised edition of *Hold On To Your Kids* (2013) states, "Like a cookie that is devoid of the nurturing elements a body needs, it (a digital device) is not only empty food but spoils the body for food it does need".

Screens have come to act as a compensation for the frustrated attachment needs of both adults and especially children. The digital revolution is here to stay whether I want it or not. These tools do have a place in our lives but it leaves me with the question: How do we create the conditions for the digital world to serve us and not destroy families and communities? I don't want to read the postings of my adult children nor my young grandchildren or to know them through Facebook, Twitter or Linkedin. I truly want to know THEM not about them.

So kids, park your phones at the door, come chat with me.

Journal: March entry

(Journal entries are shared among Neufeld Faculty)

I think that guilt nicely moves us around the wheel of frustration. Today, I received a call saying we couldn't use the Retirement Residence for Saturday's *Facing the Dragon* seminar. My first thought was that I wanted to give up on these seminars, they are too much work. I felt shame thinking about all the people who were expecting to attend the presentation and anger at those who had promised the space to me. I sat for a moment stunned - then all of a sudden guilt led me to my sense of responsibility for all those who were coming. I was stuck, I couldn't think of another venue which was suitable. Once I touched that place inside of me that is so vulnerable, I could feel the frustration that was being held in by shame, anger and guilt. Grief came quickly about something else not going my way. I accepted the guilt, grieved my loss of venue, took a deep breath and had a vision of the new Child Care Centre on Gordon Street South. I was on the phone, booked a room, signed the contract and contacted everyone within three hours. Guilt as an emotion happens to us; it is evolutionary, we have no choice in experiencing it unless we run from facing the futility of vulnerability (which is of course is the

dragon). We confuse evolutionary design with motivation. Perfection does motivate because it can never be achieved. Guilt breeds acceptance and resilience. To accept oneself is to feel the guilt.

April entry

I love THE book *"Why We Get Sick"*. Yesterday in my seminar "*Facing the Dragon: Making Sense of Stressed Out Kids, Parents and Teachers*", I wound some of Nesse and Williams' (p.116-117) evolutionary thinking around Gordon's while supporting the two with some of the latest neuroscience. People who come to my seminars (mostly academics from the University and young well-educated parents) comment that they appreciate that there is some scientific thinking that substantiates Gordon's paradigm. The more I use other references too, the more credible I think Gordon's message becomes (to my community). It seems more and more that my job is to be a conduit through which information (Gordon's paradigm) must flow. I love the stories (quite an accumulation) that I have from my own life to support Gordon's brilliance. I love it too, that the current thinking of other brilliant minds is helping to anchor Gordon's joining of the dots (although I am fully aware that no one has taken relationship to the depth Gordon has).

"Consensual Parenting" is an article I read in the Globe and I gagged. I feel a great deal of compassion for this uninformed young mother. I am constantly writing letters about what I read. The latest is a response to an article *"The secret to training kids to sleep"* in the April 6th, 2009 MacLean's magazine. This article was written by a young academic (a former student of David's) and his wife who are both developmental psychologists. Eeuw! I felt so squeamish when I read it that I had to put fingers to the keyboard. I'll post my letter to the Editor on the Campus when I get a chance.

May entry

During Saturday's collegial Support Forum, it was my intention to seek both your support and insight. Glitches in technology left me speechless but not content. For those of you who have the time or interest I send to you my thinking.

Forwarding the Neufeld paradigm is far more commitment and work than I ever imagined. I am trying to keep the whole (end result) in mind while working on the individual parts to foster change. I realize this is not an "either/or" situation as I make suggestions to consider the value of implementing some of the thinking into our systems that manage both the

care and education of our children. It is "both/and" thinking that will equip educators and child care providers with the conceptual tools to access relationships in which children can thrive.

After analyzing my decision to reach out to key players in the systems or organizations that manage our children, I disagree with myself on taking this course of action. Marshall McLuhan said, "We shape our tools and afterwards our tools shape us". Incorporation of the tools into the stance we take comes only through practice, refinement, and experience. Representatives from four systems with whom I have met and introduced Dr. Neufeld's concepts, suggesting his book or downloading appropriate DVD's cannot find a place in which his position might fit in their organization, at this time. All have said that their organization uses only evidence-based practices and they must be careful not to "position" or align themselves with one paradigm or another.

My belief is that all humans are capable of changing their stance if we can allow ourselves to change the tools and experiences that we use. Changing tools develops our thinking capacity.

For now, I haven't found a creative solution to fostering an appreciation of the pivotal role relationships take in learning and behaviour.

Healthy responses to the frustration that comes from experiencing something that is not working swirl in my head. I can attempt to change things, accept things as they are now or adapt creatively to situations that cannot change. My mission is perhaps a little grandiose. I want to be a part of shaping the world for a better future. For children, I cannot accept that life is about accepting unattractive and unpleasant trade-offs. The solution lies in my ability to reserve judgment and to have patience until I gather more of what I need to know to carry out my intentions. The answer lies in a place that I haven't thought of yet.

The whole educational system is perseverating. Principals are quoted in our local newspapers saying that our current zero-tolerance policy for bullying is not working. Children are more aggressive than ever. We have police officers in our high schools, young women in our high schools are making sexual harassment charges against their peers, young men are using the highly sexually charged lyrics from rap music to alarm themselves and others. This is a war zone in which our children are trying to survive. The Board of Education is doing the best it can in crisis management.

Last Friday, while reading our local paper, an advertisement for a Psychologist caught my eye. This is a six-month position which is intended to attract a person who has knowledge of behaviour assessment and interventions which will support the suspension/expulsion program for students Grade 6 – 12. The psychologist is to address problematic student behaviour and to assist the students in developing the social/emotional skills necessary for school re-entry. The Director of Education to whom possible candidates apply is a woman I spoke with in August, who assured me she is familiar with Dr. Neufeld's work. She explained to me that because the paradigm does not have evidence-based research to back it, her hands are tied. I feel saddened that what has not worked is seen as a better way than introducing teachers to all the possibilities that unfold when the lens of attachment is used. For now, I will remain patient, knowing there must be regression in growth. My aspirations do not have to change. I will wait until the context is more fertile so that I can carry out my intentions.

Trying to establish a context by having Gordon here for an evening presentation has been another exercise in frustration. Late in August, the Upper Grand Board of Education considered extending an invitation but their funding has been directed into educating parents about Cyber-Bullying. Both the YM/YWCA and Ontario Early Years Centre do not want to be seen to be promoting one paradigm over another. Family and Childrens' Services, Canadian Mental Health and the Catholic School Board provided contact people for me to call. I have spoken with the contact people who are in charge of both professional and parent development. At this time, a new lens through which we could understand our children is still closed to a presentation by Gordon. However, I have been invited to volunteer to speak at two small gatherings in March.

Mindful Confessions

This journal entry is in response to a question which I have asked myself many times during this stormy, bleak winter of 2008: "Why am I doing what I'm doing when I could be sitting on a beach with other retired folk reviewing my achievements?"..
I am very aware that I am not a winter person. I much prefer the springtime with the promise of new beginnings. Yet most winters, I experience a time of recession in which I retreat to think about my life - redefining, reassessing and rebuilding my motivation for growth. It is interesting that all three of my pregnancies took on a long gestation through the fall and winter and produced new life in the spring. My formal commitment to David through marriage vows was declared publicly in March. What is it about spring?
In an earlier journal entry I was experiencing feelings of dissonance, feelings of futility and feelings of foul frustration. Representatives from four systems with whom I met and introduced Neufeld thinking couldn't find a place in which his position might fit without some evidence of the paradigm's effectiveness. After writing my rant, I grieved for many days in the dark hole of a snow storm. Grieving that I had courageously reached out to what seemed to be unwelcoming systems to offer new ways of seeing

stuck children. My profound sadness about doors not opening as quickly as I thought they should led me to an insight that shook me up. I needed to provide more space for the "systems" to think about what I was offering. Maybe it was me who needed to cool her jets. Admittedly, I was feeling the void of not being chosen to lead the County away from what I saw as obvious blindness.
I want to lead from my deepest sense of being – honouring and evoking ways of knowing from my heart – to embrace the essence of who people are and to invite them to be fully human in my presence. I must slow down and experience this paradigm in all facets of my life. I must let go of right and wrong answers and illusions of control so that I can listen to my heart and intuition. My desire is to be able to adapt and to soak up this futility of fulfilling my agenda on how things should work.
There is an emergent new world struggling to be born; a new map that will recover a life-affirming system for sustaining the preciousness of family. The school system will change after the landscape of the family changes. Our world is multi-faceted, multi-dimensional, multi-directional and multi-generational. Inviting the grandparents, parents and their children to embrace the invisible strings among them will make room for all of us to stay interdependent. A

community womb for fostering this new creation will come together when the time is ready.

Even considering that beach in Florida sounds pretty far-fetched today but we are one day closer to spring. This is the springtime of my calling – I have already had a career. My decision is to continue on this path with the next generation (my grandchildren) in mind. I can see that their future is being born in everything I do or not do and it can't happen if I'm celebrating my past. This new generation holds the seeds to sustainability.

My contact at the Wellington Catholic School Board whom I met with in December, then wrote a proposal for in January, contacted me yesterday to say that my proposal had been accepted at the School Board level and only requires Ministry approval which he is hopeful will happen this month. There just might be enough grace and compassion left in me to forgive myself for what I saw as blindness.

To choose a life in which I keep learning;

To find reflective, quiet times where I can rest from the static of that which surrounds and bombards me;

To accept that this is my calling – to forward the paradigm – this follows a career;

To commit honesty, goodness, generosity, and compassion to the mix that is my future legacy.

It is important:

To be visible in the world and speak my voice and hope over cynicism;

To decide that this is the paradigm that I want to put my name on;

The Gift of Guilt – a Necessary Virtue

Guilt reveals the attachment conscience. The development of a safe emotional relationship is directed by an adult who yearns to make things work by taking responsibility for the pursuit and preservation of the relationship with a child. Relationships are never the responsibility of a child. Often, parents say, "If I could only find a reason (they often mean "a diagnosis") for my child's behaviour, I would feel better and be able to cope with him/her". Labelling a child with a diagnosis does not help to understand the roots of the relationship with you. When we change the idea of responsibility or blame, then we don't feel so much guilt and nothing changes. Guilt is a vulnerable experience and if it is not felt because we are too defended and afraid of being vulnerable then the child is blamed and everything stays the same in the dynamic of the parent-child hierarchy. Too often, we want our children to fit into the boxes we construct for them. It would be so much easier for us, if our kids reached for the potential that we see for them. Expectations can make us all prisoners of the ideal instead of the real. When we allow guilt to help us to see that we are expecting something different than the reality of what is, we are led into a new emotional space which allows us to accept differences. Compromises and challenges in the family help us all to grow into evolved people.

Guilt is not your fault but is there to move you to take responsibility. The emotion of guilt is inevitable and cannot be escaped, without a cost. Guilt develops on top of our frustration of things not going our way and moves us to a place of acceptance. When we are able to grieve the loss of not having the child we anticipated, we are in a better position to parent the child who did come to us through biology or adoption. Reaching futility through guilt transforms many parent-child relationships. Without guilt, we would be living in a moral vacuum. There would be no consequences to our thoughts and actions and our role as a parent would become increasingly meaningless.Don't run away from your feelings of guilt. If guilt is absent, there is no opportunity for grace, nor forgiveness and for seeing with new eyes. When shaming guilt (i.e. "Look what you made me do!". or "Look at what you have done to deliberately make my life miserable!".) is used to discipline children, it exploits their immaturity. In the end, using these powerful emotions against a child in order to control him/her creates neuroses.Find your frustration and in your tears around what can't be, you will find your release, your grace.

Accepting oneself is to experience the guilt inside. The attachment conscience is essential in looking at guilt; inviting it to exist and allowing it to transform us into being the parent our child needs us to be. We are formed by our first primary attachment. Whatever a mother/father cannot invite in herself/himself cannot be invited in a child.

When guilt is thwarted, resentment grows and woundedness builds. Guilt is a gift, use it well!

Parenthood

" Attachment is about who we are with children not with what we do. It isn't very complicated but it does involve parents, teachers and child-care providers taking responsibility for the work of relationship..."

Attachment Parenting Not a Recipe

(Letter to the Editor, Guelph Mercury, September 19, 2012)

"Toddler Talk" columnist Brianne Collechio made a valiant attempt to describe all "sides" of attachment in her recent column. However, she has left out the most critical piece. Attachment is not a style of parenting with a recipe for how to parent. Attachment was best understood by Sir John Bowlby, a British psychologist whose research validated the impact of safe, emotional relationships on the development of children. To-day, his relational work is supported by both neuroscience and developmental psychology. The extensive research from neuroscientists Dr. Allan Schore and Dr. Bessel van der Kolk show that children who are in safe, emotional relationships with the adults responsible for their care, carry less worry and reach their full potential.

Attachment is about who we are with children not with what we do. It isn't very complicated but it does involve parents, teachers and child-care providers taking responsibility for the work of relationship, thereby giving children the freedom necessary to develop into emotionally and intellectually strong people.

Connecting Suggestions for Parents

(Response to the organizer of a workshop for parents and teachers)

I was thinking for the hand-out that we could start with simple but often forgotten attachment manners:

Smile

Have a twinkle in your eye

Always greet your child when s/he comes home or walks past you

Tell endearing stories about your child as a baby

Make your child feel delicious

Tickle, pull a toe, rub his head, touch her back to connect

Remember you want your child to want to be with you

Point out what is working for the child

Remind that the relationship with you is forever

Find something that is lovable in your child

Enjoy each other

Let the clouds of emotion roll on by

Remember their brain is still under construction and needs some coaching

Remember to remember - help your kids to exercise their memory by giving them lots of practice at recalling important events: in the car, at the dinner table, wherever…

This is a start off the top of my head. Is this what you had in mind?

Warmly,

Susan

Parenthood: giving when the well feels dry

Love and support, given unconditionally inside a nurturing relationship, is what every parent strives for after making the decision to raise a child; this is the essence of parenthood. For the past thirty years, parents have been increasingly overwhelmed by all of the programs and activities being offered by organizations convinced they have the answer to bringing children to their full potential. In a society which values athletic skills, *not too much intelligence*, limitless sociability and the latest in technology, we have lost the relationship with children that previous generations took for granted. Parenting has become a set of skills to be followed along lines recommended by experts. Today's parenting strategies are not getting the return on the investment that many expected. With the increase in childhood and adolescent mental health and behavioural problems, the understanding of parenthood has become infinitely more important than the search for any plan of action.

Not long ago, I overheard a young father and his two sons (ages 4 & 6) chatting together in a small coffee shop early on a Saturday morning. "Tommy," the father said to the four year old (whose face lit up when he was addressed), "you are going to play hockey this year, learn to skate fast, stick handle and score lots of goals. Soon you'll earn a place on a rep team and be able to travel to hockey games every weekend. You'll probably be spotted by an NHL hockey recruiter and be able to play pro hockey and earn millions of dollars, a year". As the plan unfolded, Tommy's face became increasingly glummer. His eyes filled up with tears and he said, "But Dad, I just want to shoot the puck around with you". Tommy's Dad played minor hockey and he always had aspirations of becoming a big league star. His father (Tommy's grandfather) had no time to take him to games because he was committed to working the demanding hours his advertising agency expected. How he longed to play sports - or did he? What Tommy's Dad was not aware of was that he was still yearning for a relationship with his own father. Thinking that being a star would provide the fulfillment which he lacked, Tommy's Dad focused on shaping his son into an all-Canadian icon. At four, Tommy's instincts could still experience the force of the attraction to his Daddy. What Tommy wanted was for his Dad to orient him in time and space, to have similar interests, to make some room for him to matter and to keep him safe. In this moment, it was clear that all of Tommy's energy was going into finding his bearings. He became very anxious and slugged his little brother. A tousle followed. The situation in the coffee shop was more than the Dad could handle and he yelled at both boys telling them they could never again come out with him for breakfast on a Saturday morning; they were both grounded in their rooms until dinner time. The boys left with their father in a cloud of destructive energy.

This is one of many situations that is played out on any Saturday morning. Parents intend to connect with their children but unwittingly trip over some hidden impediment from their past. This hurdle blinds them to their children's longing for the warmth of an invitation to exist, just as they are.

How can we get this message across to our children? Experts try to convince us that there is a skill set that can be acquired

but exercising skills without a relationship is the difference between parenting and parenthood.

Motherhood : 1970 and 2011

A recent article (Toronto *Globe and Mail*, May 6/11) argues that in 2011 motherhood "feels overwhelming", and "there's incredible pressure" as though the mother is totally responsible for the child's social and psychological life in addition to their health and welfare. In contrast, the author describes an earlier time when mothers cooked what they knew how to cook, put their kids "out to air" while they did the house work, and sent their children off to neighbor-hood schools and recreation centers for whatever lessons they took. Mothers did not expect their children to become prodigies and the author suggests that in the disco era being a mom might have been more carefree.

Interestingly, mothers now spend about the same time with their children as did the moms of 40 years ago despite all of the activities they now take responsibility for. Where does the time come from? Probably from time spent on housework, on leisure time activities, on relationships with their children's father and on time for sleep. Certainly the lack of sleep which modern moms report has had a huge impact. In a 1970 survey 12% of British moms said their lack of sleep was wrecking their sex lives; in 2005 this figure had skyrocketed to 66%! Worrying about feeding their children the right foods has also bloomed. In 1978 only 30% of mothers could name any food which their families should avoid; in 2010 concerns about serving the right food had soared to include 80% of mothers.

The shift in what parenting and family have meant over these years is perhaps best illustrated by the observation that in 1992 64% of teenagers ate dinner with their family. By 2005 this figure had dropped to 35%.

The article refers to the experience of a mature woman in her 60's who had raised three children in the 70s and who recently adopted a seven year-old daughter. When asked which decade she preferred in terms of being a mother - balancing the pros and cons, weighing the convenience of a microwave compared with moms who could still laugh together over their "bratty" kids – she replied with a laugh, "A mom in the seventies...with more money."

Not enough Parental Support

Re: Article in *Toronto Star*, Jan 11, 2010.

Invest in Kids, an organization which deals with research and public education has demonstrated that the more parents feel confident and the more they understand child development, the more positive their behaviour is towards their kids. They play and laugh with their children; praise them and are less likely to scold, punish or shame their kids.

However, many who were involved in a sample of 2,500 parents who had a spouse and a child under the age of 5 report that in many ways they lack the support they feel they need. About half of all of these parents felt they had support from their own parents and from other family members and friends, but only 1 in 4 parents felt a high level of support from their neighbourhood communities. Perhaps more disturbing is that only about half of the parents felt highly supported by their partner.

In short, too few felt highly supported by those who were closest to them and they turned instead, to the on-line community to find programs and drop-ins where they could feel connected. The impact of these drop-in centres and the contacts which are made there can be massive. As one father said, "I feel that the importance of being a dad is really undervalued", but by becoming a part of network: it makes me feel supported and that no matter what happens there's someone I can turn to." Internet support groups are an example of peer orientation which is the engine behind parenting mythology.

An Ode to my Mother

Joyful, joyful, we adore Thee,
God of glory, Lord of love;
Hearts unfold like flowers before
Thee, opening to the sun above,
Melt the clouds of sin and
sadness; drive the dark of doubt
away;
Giver of immortal gladness, fill us
with light of day!

Words by Henry J. van Dyke
(1907); Music by Ludwig von
Beethoven (1824)

Today, I would like to pay tribute
to my mother.

In North American society where
the emotional right brain is
encouraged to be suppressed,
the celebration of the logical left
brain has led us to an increase in
specialization; technicalization
of knowledge; increased
bureaucratization, and a lack of
respect for judgment and skill
acquired through experience
(Schore, 2012).

Before the days of thinking of
parenting as a skill, a technique
or a recipe, I was born to
Florence L. Dafoe on November
09, 1948. Stored in her right
brain were all of the unconscious
processes and emotional

experiences necessary to be the
mother that I needed her to be.
Attachment is defined as the
interactive regulation of states of
biological synchronicity between
and within organisms (Schore,
2000). My mother's soothing
(her gaze, her soft voice and her
gentle reassuring touch) was able
to down-regulate my
negative, autonomically aroused
fear states because she was
unconsciously attuned to my
needs. In the times that I showed
interest and excitement, she had
the uncompromised ability to
take me into states of joy
thereby up-regulating positive
emotions in play states. How do I
know this now? I have watched
her with my children and their
children, my grandchildren. The
emotional regulator of the family,
she has provided the
components of healthy self-
esteem and emotional regulation
to three children, nine
grandchildren and seven great-
grandchildren.

Currently, neuroscience has
informed us that attachment
histories are affectively burnt
into our right brain and become
implicit relational knowledge.
The right hemisphere holds
representations of the emotional
states of events that have been

experienced by the individual. When we encounter a familiar scenario, representations of past emotional experiences are retrieved by the right hemisphere and incorporated into the reasoning process (Schore, 2012). In many relationships, we are at high risk to project a non-verbal, unconscious memory on an innocent person as a way to lessen our attachment anxiety. Primary mother-infant relations are stored non-verbally forever, in the right hemisphere. Early experience shapes genetic expression and shapes structures that have a lifelong impact on our most vital areas of learning: attachment, emotional self-regulation and self-esteem. These three spheres of learning establish our abilities to connect with others, to cope with stress, to feel loveable and to believe that we have value.

Given how little control I had over my early experience and that I could have been born to anyone regardless of competence, I am grateful my brain building was not left to chance. Inside my mother's house, her relationship with me drove my brain development. Bowlby (1988) supported by

Neufeld (2004) assure us that healthy attachment behaviour is based on a need for safety and a secure base. Now, neuroscience is clear that attachment is the essential matrix for creating a right brain that can regulate its own internal and external relationships.

Our *in utero* and our early postnatal interpersonal world shape and mold the individual we are to become (Schore, 2012). My mother likes to tell people that she taught me everything that I know. Indeed, it is our early attachment relationship that shaped my internal psychic structure so that I could work with the right brains of people for over fifty years.

Professionally, for more than twenty years as a family therapist and as a consultant to parents and teachers for six years, my work of equipping people with the resources to make sense of each other and their children has been all about what I learned from my mother. Relationships are not a left brain activity.

Today, the day my daughter handed in her Master's thesis which focuses on mothering in a professional left brain world, my ode to my mother involves my gratitude that she gave me and my daughter the tools to cultivate the soil for others to grow into their full potential.

Thanks Mom, you have made a difference in the lives of many generations past, present and future. I love you forever.

References

Bowlby, J. (1988). *A secure base.* New York: Basic Books.

Cozolino, L. (2010). *The Neuroscience of Psychotherapy.* New York: W.W. Norton and Company.

Neufeld, G. (2004). *Hold On To Your Kids.* Toronto: Random House.

Schore, A.N. (2012). *The Science and Art of Psychotherapy.* New York: W.W. Norton and Company.

The Parent-Child Relationship Requires: Acceptance, Grace and Action with Eloquence

Relationship is in the expression in your eyes when your child looks into them.

Relationship is in your voice as your child makes meaning of the tone.

Relationship is the message your child receives from your touch. Relationship is in the scent you transmit during an interaction with your child.

Relationship is what your child tastes when s/he is with you.

Relationship is wanting to talk, walk, sit, laugh, dress and be like you.

Relationship is feeling a sense of belonging and mattering.

Relationship is believing that your love knows no hesitation, no start and no finish.

Relationship is the desire to share all secrets and trusting the secrets aren't too

much to bear and will be held in safe keeping.

Parenting in the News

Parenting has been in the news a lot recently! The Huffington Post now has a parenting section... the Christian Science Monitor's most recent edition's cover commanded: "Let the Children Play". I noted with a chuckle that EVERY photograph was of a child with, in, or on, expensive plastic and metal, branded toys; almost every shot was taken indoors, and not one of the photos was taken in nature. I wrote a letter pointing out the virtues of simple free play... we'll see if they publish it.

Parenting in our time:

This issue (Jan/Feb, 2012) of the prestigious *Psychotherapy Networker* asks the provocative question: "Are Parents Obsolete?". In his Editorial Rich Simon notes: "Never before in history have parents had to bring up kids in an environment so inimical to parental authority, so family unfriendly, as 21st century American society. In the face of invasive, family-destabilizing external forces, including the omnipresent Internet, an overbearing and demanding school system, ubiquitous drugs and alcohol, ruthless consumer marketing to kids, endemic bullying, a family-supplanting youth culture, not to mention widespread economic uncertainty, 'authoritative parenting' hardly stands a chance."

I think most of us feel the buren of the truth of Rich Simon's observations at many time during out parenting years. Parenting is really a struggle, often! What hope is there for family life, for children and for childhood?

Proposal for Therapists

Simon continues:

We (therapists) need to get out more, go to school meetings, hold public workshops, and do our part in helping to establish "communities of practice" around the critical issue of taking back legitimate adult authority for the raising of kids in a society so dedicated to subverting it. While parents may sometimes feel obsolete, the need of all children and adolescents for parental love and authority isn't, and never will be. Parents just need a little help from their friends to reclaim what's rightfully theirs.

Parents Get Stuck Too

A recent article in the Toronto Globe and Mail reminded me of the futility of parents who force their children to take sides in a marital dispute. In this particular case, a young boy has been referred to a special U.S clinic where he will be "deprogrammed" using a "private remedy" to deal with "the disease of parental alienation".

The father, during acrimonious divorce proceedings, pursued an assault charge against the mother. As a result, the boy, then ten years old, had to testify in criminal court against his mother. The father gained custody of the child and refused him access to his mother. The child's relationship to his father became so intertwined that the father's beliefs about the mother were transmitted to the child. Over a period of time the father convinced his son that he would be harmed by continuing any relationship with his mother. The distraught mother recently resumed court action requesting sole custody. The judge noted that "the age of a child is no reason to justify a lost

opportunity to know and benefit from both of the child's parents". He assumed that the child would need treatment and that professionals with specialized credentials must be called in to rectify the situation.

The financial cost of court, lawyers, psychologists and a clinic which works with "alienated children" is enormous. The power of the parents to anchor their child has been overlooked. This child is further burdened with undergoing intensive psychotherapy in order to bring his thinking in line with the judge's while his parents sit unaware that it was their defended vulnerability that created the problem in the first place. The parents are asking their child to do their work. Children should never be asked to the something which is an adult's responsibility.

Divorcing parents do not intentionally hurt their children with their foul frustration over the losses incurred from an unsatisfactory union. The futility of what hasn't worked often doesn't sink in and the grief required to see the future clearly gets clouded with the automatic response of the brain. When the pain of loss (in this case sharing a child with a perceived enemy) becomes so unbearable that it threatens to overwhelm the capacity to function, there is an unconscious mechanism that is automatically put into gear. This numbing out, tuning out, backing out mechanism exists in the brain so that humans can endure trauma that would otherwise be catastrophic. The consequence of this numbing out mechanism is that there is a dulling of emotional awareness and a lost capacity to feel emotional pain or to sense another's emotional turmoil. Parents can get stuck in their vulnerability and end up trying to cope with life's static in the same way that fragile, sensitive children do by numbing out, tuning out and backing out of relationships.

This numbing which blocks or distorts incoming information into the frontal cortex leaves a by-product of free floating frustration which can turn foul and erupt in very alarming behaviour as we see with this particular father. For children, the eruption of foul frustration is often referred to as "bullying". Bullies are the most fragile among all human-beings.

Working with the parents, helping them to understand the damage they are imposing on their young son is the best bet. This child needs to hear from both his parents that it is O.K. to have a relationship with the other. The parents have the power to anchor this boy.

The use of parental power is very evident. The father brought the boy into relationship with him and then abused his parental authority in the hierarchy. Instead of allowing the womb of the relationship to be a place in which he could transmit culture, teach values and foster development, the father turned the child against his own mother to support his position against her and to gain esteem in his son's eyes.

Parents get stuck in their own issues and unintentionally create great angst for their children. My work as a Parent Consultant is often heart-wrenching. Seeing parents who insist that their children's' behaviour must change, before they will enter a relationship with them, stands at the top of the list of parental sins. Children can't make changes just because we tell them to. As soon as a child sniffs out a disconnect with us or sees that s/he is in charge of contact, the child will experience this as too much of a burden and turn to a teddy bear, a blanket, a pet or peers. They will seek out someone or something else with whom or with which to feel emotionally safe. We have gone too far with our expectations for children.

We have forgotten that it is we the parents who shield our children from the chaos of society. Children must be able to depend on the responsible adults in their lives.

In North American society there is a prevailing fear of dependence and coddling. The result is that parents are forcing independence. As in the case of parent alienation which I spoke about earlier, the father abused his power and successfully attempted to inculcate his ideas into the child. He encouraged the child to speak as an independent thinker at age 10 in a court case against his mother. The father pushed for this independence and the original judge accepted that these were the child's feelings and beliefs. Parents cannot alone create independence.

Nature has a huge part in the unfolding of a child's developmental destiny. Children become their own person spontaneously. The wiring for the process is in place but independence can only happen when a child's dependency needs are met. Dependency and independence co-exist in maturity. Like dependence on food, we remain dependent on contact and closeness to those with whom we feel emotionally safe.

For all children, parents must believe in the developmental process and assist in moving impediments out of the way of their child reaching his/her full human potential. In this case of child alienation, both the parents and the court system are stuck in their own fragility. This has led to unintentional blindness.

Psychotherapy and Parenting: Kissin' Cousins

The goal of therapy is to integrate and balance various left and right hemisphere processing networks. Neural structures and responses to stimuli are determined by multigenerational experiences. The amygdala which is the central hub for processing fear is fully developed by 6 months of age and is influenced by the mother's levels of stress hormones during pregnancy and the child's life. The mother has likely inherited her stress responses from her mother and her mother from her mother. This legacy of the amygdala continues to pair emotional conditioning with incoming sensory information through the generations.

Fear is learned by pairing any thought, feeling or sensation to any anxious stimulus (Cozolino, 2013). The amygdala's function is to bring us to caution and learning to be anxious can be passed on from generation to another. Sustained anxiety stress results in high levels of cortisol being produced. This results in another part of the brain, the hippocampus, which is involved in memory being severely affected and this puts us at risk for learning difficulties. Behaviour is shaped by fear and the amygdala has the potential to continue to pair any

stimulus, (even physical affection or praise) with fear. Reinforcement of the connections among neurons is an unconscious process which often leads to avoidance of the stimulus which created the original anxiety. This avoidance is a short-term attempt to reduce the anxiety but it actually prevents any neural integration which would be necessary to overcome the disturbing reactions. Anxiety becomes generalized and fear is perpetuated.

Children's emotions are naturally rapidly changing and overwhelming. It is the underdeveloped brain that is responsible for their inability to control affect regulation. As children mature, the middle portions of the frontal cortex expand and extend their fibres down into the limbic (emotional) system and the brain stem. Over time children gradually gain increased capacity to regulate their emotions and to self soothe. When there is difficulty, a therapist or an attuned parent can facilitate the process.

Psychotherapy, like parenting, can help to provide an emotionally supportive environment in which integration of: the emotional experience of alarm/ fear; the sensations; the coping behaviours and the thoughts about the fear can begin. Talking about the upset activates areas of the rational left hemisphere along with the emotional centres of the right hemisphere and clients become aware of their inner and outer worlds as they are "being heard and known" by their therapist. Through this process a narrative develops that serves to process the fear. Healing occurs through the neural integration of the networks in the brain.

Hooking ourselves into someone else's rational cortex (left hemisphere) and their emotional centres in the right hemisphere modulates anxiety for those who can't regulate their emotions on their own and becomes the foundation from which brain development can proceed.

Recessionary Parenting

(Adapted from a *Globe and Mail* article)

"If my husband and I lost our jobs, and my kid wanted to sign up for a $1200 hockey program", says a Calgary college instructor, "I'd borrow the money. I'd take a loan. That makes no objective sense, it's just me, being warped, but I feel an enormous pressure every day."

As financial markets shrivel, a similar paranoia has gripped many parents. They are afraid that their infants will suddenly become hobos if they fail to give them every opportunity despite the financial pressures which providing these might create. They pay for or finance: dance classes special driving programs, imported enrichment workbooks, computer programs to teach six-year olds how to manage their money and countless other aides to education and development (or so the parents believe). The merit of one's ability as a parent is being measured by how many extra classes can be given to the child.

Child raising has become mechanized and complex and frequently smacks of a projection of the parents' needs. The simple and free resources to help one's child are being ignored or discounted. One expert finds it incomprehensible that six-year olds should be staring at computer screens to learn how to save and grow their allowance rather than digging up twitchy earthworms.

To which I would add, "It isn't what you do for your child it's who you are to him or her".

Reclaiming Our Kids: Relationship Matters

We are trying to do all the right things for our kids but recent University of Minnesota research points out that young children spend more time in cars going to and from activities than they do sitting at the dinner table, involved in the simple ritual of the family meal. By trying to give our kids everything, we have overlooked the importance of surrendering ourselves to the art and science of building and sustaining a relationship with them.

With all good intentions, following the advice of experts, we have managed to cut ourselves off from our kids and thrust them into activities to fill them up. Working with parents, coaches and teachers, I am learning that many adults are so anxious about doing "the wrong thing" that they have become paralyzed. The contradictory advice which has been offered to parents over the past thirty years has contributed to the confusion about what to do. Looking for a one-size-fits-all theory, parents buy into one approach only to find in a short time that there is another theory which has superseded the first.

Theory has proven to be ineffectual. The modern self-esteem industry which results in every child being told that they are "special" just for "being a person" has become just as hollow as tough love, consequences, time-outs and rewards. Medicating, punishing, providing alibis (diagnoses) for "spoiled" and "undisciplined children" hasn't made a difference either.

Parents, teachers, counsellors and child-care providers are stretched to the limit. We do spend more time with our kids than in past generations but when we look at what we are doing during this time, a troubling picture unfolds. Often, it seems we are engaged in parallel but separate activities. Mother may be supervising her five-year-old's supper while simultaneously arranging a meeting for the next day; brother is emailing several friends while talking with yet another friend on the phone; Dad is looking up from his computer every ten minutes or so to say to whomever will listen, "It's almost bedtime!".

There is no way to get to know children if we are doing something else. I remember clearly, many years ago, one of my children walking over to where I was, down on my hands and knees, washing a floor. Carefully, he put his hand on my shoulder, bent over to look into my eyes and asked timidly, "When can you stop being so busy and just talk to 'your little boy'?". This was a heartfelt response from my son who was desperate to be seen, heard, and touched, to feel that he mattered, that he belonged to me, that I loved him and that he was truly known by me.

When children aren't in relationship with an adult who wants to know them inside out, and to protect them from all the expectations burdening them, there will always be something else to fill the dark void. Parents, teachers and caregivers are floundering around in their own moral confusion but it doesn't have to stay that way; relationships are the answer.

Rest

"Rest is a place or condition in which the child does not feel driven: driven to please, to succeed, to take part in, or to interact."

Children need rest as well as sleep

What does the research say?

In the new field of neuroscience one of the most powerful tools in use is the fMRI (functional Magnetic Resonance Imaging). This procedure (it looks like an X-ray is being taken) lets us look inside the skull and see changes in blood flow in the brain as problems are tackled. We can also measure the electrical activity of different parts of the brain. The evidence being collected from labs around the world is that sleep and rest are two different processes.

During sleep, facts, word-meanings and disconnected fragments of memories are churned in blocks of sixty to ninety minutes several times a night (periods associated with Rapid Eye Movements). On a fMRI, the visual cortex and hippocampus light up indicating that these two parts of the brain are at work. Between these work periods the brain reviews recent "real" events and memories of the past. Free from deliberate activity during wakeful periods of rest fMRIs show our brains are extremely active; much more so than when we focus on routine tasks. The seat of our daydreams appears to be the 'default network' - a region of the brain that remains active when we

rest or are not engaged in a focused task, but which switches off when we need to concentrate.

How much rest does our child need?

How much sleep does our child need? How much sleep do you, as a parent need (and "How will I ever get it?" you ask)? Let's talk about the difference between sleep and rest. As a culture, we have lost the structures that once provided rest and the wisdom that told us that children needed rest. We tend to keep children engaged, busy, involved and stimulated rather than provide space for rest. Rest is at the root of growth and is at the core of Dr. Gordon Neufeld's relational paradigm.

What is Rest?

Rest happens when the mind is free of stress, when it can create daydreams, luxuriate in creative play, go to other universes or simply throw up random ideas and images which might be remembered or perhaps not. When children are resting, they are freed from the hunger of attachment; they feel secure in the comfort a parent provides; they can experience desire and fear at the same time and they can live in a place where there might not be any answers. Life just is! Rest is a place or condition in which the child does not feel driven: driven to please, to succeed, to take part in, or to interact. How do we lead children to a place where they are not anxious to please, not on a constant quest for approval, for contact, for value? We can free them by taking charge of their relationships and by being fully present for them, inviting them to be with us and letting them know that we have faith that they will grow up and reach their full potential.

Anxious children do not learn

When children are preoccupied with making decisions about what to do, what to eat, who to play with, even which nursery school they should go to, they develop a sense that they are responsible for their own needs and this creates anxiety. In this state the body produces cortisol - a powerful hormone which interferes with development. High cortisol levels in the brain can interfere with the child's ability to integrate learning, to focus, to get along with others and to experience a sense of emotional safety. Where does sleep fit into this picture? We need sleep to allow our physical body to heal and to grow; that is a fact of life and everyone has known this without the benefit of research. What we didn't know, until recently, was that if we didn't rest while we were sleeping (or didn't get some periods of rest during the day) we simply don't learn as well as we might. Resting allows the various parts of the

brain to "talk" to one another. Not only do they talk, they engage in a kind of dance in which they get into step with one another and when this happens, new material and experiences can be woven together into new arrangements so that they are more easily recalled and used in the future.

How do rest and sleep affect your child differently?

Sleep will allow physical development and physical maturation to occur; but your child needs rest to benefit from learning opportunities which may have come by during the day. Naps and daydreams are ways in which the brain gives itself room to develop. The child who dozes off during a class or while watching TV may not be disinterested or even over-tired; her brain may simply be taking a few moments to block out the world outside the skull while allowing the brain to process what's already been taken in. (College students who nap frequently do better on academic tests than those who cram!) Hamlet said, "To sleep, perchance to dream ... " to which might be added, " ... and rest as best we can".

Growth thru Rest

The greatest challenge to any parent is to bring a child to a place of rest. Not necessarily to a place of sleep, although sleep promotes physical growth if there is psychological freedom from worry. Rest is described by Dr. Gordon Neufeld, as being a still point where children are no longer moved to pursue closeness to their parents, no longer stuck in trying to make things work that do not work, and when children are able to live with a coexistence of doubts and beliefs.

Both contemporary parenting advice and learning theory miss the point by not looking at the concept of rest. Rest is absolutely the core to the developmental approach. The child emerges into the world after age five when the prefrontal cortex is hooking up, when the child can understand fairness and can take his or her turn. Credit has been given to learning social skills but it is not learning that allows this to happen. It is development. Senselessly, both pre-school and junior kindergarten programs are focused on teaching social skills when this is impossible developmentally. Children's brains are not hooked-up to permit socializing to happen until age five or six. Pre and primary school teachers would do better to focus on the relationships they have with the child instead of trying to do the impossible

by encouraging relationships among the children. Until age five or six, children are designed not to get along. Children are still learning who they are as individuals and are developmentally unable to be concerned about how they are going to fit into the social context.

In this contrived world, we miss the importance of the developmental processes of emergence and maturation. Only the child who emerges as a separate individual can be shoe-horned into a part of a larger group. In other words, the ability to be cooperative happens when a child is developmentally ready. How can we as teachers and parents facilitate this development?

Our work as human-beings is to pursue proximity or closeness to those to whom we are attached. Having proximity is a child's only hope to grow, to reach his potential. In the same way that a hungry child can never rest from pursuing food, an attachment-hungry child can never rest from pursuing attachment. Even when attachment is satiated for a young child, it is only for a few hours. During that time, a child can rest from the pursuit and in that freedom can have room to grow into maturity. How can we as teachers and parents help our children get to the place where they are not anxious to please, not in a constant hunt for closeness, for approval, for worth, for value and for recognition?

If we withhold all of the above until the child does what we want, the whole quest becomes the psychology of work rather than the psychology of rest. The child becomes responsible to fill their attachment needs through what they do for us. This is not a child's job. When the child becomes preoccupied with the hunt for attachment, he is unable to find the rest necessary to mature. Before we are asked, we must take charge of providing messages of love, specialness and acceptance to our children. Through maintaining an over-abundant supply of love, warmth, enjoyment and delight, our children will begin to trust that they can rest from the work of pursuing closeness and will be able to depend on us.

We, as parents and teachers, must communicate to our children that we believe in the child's eventual becoming, that we understand their shortcomings, that we have patience for their mistakes. Reassurances such as: "I know you'll get there"; "don't worry, it will come to you"; "it takes time to grow up" and "there's lots of time" convey a message of faith in a child's development. The acknowledgment that we know and love our children for who they are allows children to rest in who they are.

Learning to let go of what doesn't work also helps a child to mature. Parents and teacher are responsible for providing "no's", for providing structure so that a child can predict what is next, and for limit setting. When this is not what the child wants to hear, we can invite our child to their tears and hold them in the comfort of our love. Not everything in life works out the way a child would like nor can a child do everything he or she wants to do. It is the tears over what do not work that bring a child to a place of rest and subsequent resilience. When a child is able to accept questions that have no answers and can hold more than one feeling and/or one opinion at a time, s/he can rest in the "not knowing". We as parents and teachers can model our own dissonance in our discourse with our children.

Our children are suffering from overstimulation. The brain cannot endure the cultural myth that more stimulation is better. Brains need huge periods of rest or they become toxic from information overload. We tend to worry that we are not doing a good job if we are not keeping our children stimulated, engaged, involved, and busy. Parents and teachers must provide time for rest and quiet reflection or the brain will become defended and numb out. Babies in preemie nurseries usually sleep more than babies who are with their mothers in birthing rooms. Research has shown us that because of the auditory stimulation of monitors and the visual stimulation of the lights, preemies' brains numb out from the environment by increasing a sleep hormone.

Contemporary children are burdened with making far too many decisions. Parents and teachers must take back the responsibility for being the providers and therefore the decision-makers for young children. We expect children to make many choices every day, which in turn gives them the idea that they are responsible for taking care of their own needs. Responsible adults are the answers to children's needs; determining what will be eaten for meals, what time is bed-time, where the family will spend their leisure time and what activities are appropriate. Children must not be called upon to make these decisions. Parents and teachers are their children's best bet.

Restlessness is on the rise among our children. We must create structures that can provide rest in a chaotic world. Most parents and teachers believe, that if they weren't doing their job their children would never grow up. In actual fact, if the context of attachment is provided, the child grows up just fine. As parents and teachers, we need to rest from working so hard at making our children grow up and let them unfold as nature intended - inside our shield.

Teaching and Schooling

"Providing kindergarten and day-care
'opportunities' for young children will
do absolutely nothing to improve
children's social skills, mental health or
academic performance."

Full-day Kindergarten

(Letter to the Editor, *Guelph Mercury*, June 16, 2009)

The greatest cost of implementing the Pascal/McGuinty proposals for full-day kindergarten in Ontario may well be emotional, not financial. Jonas Himmelstrand, addressing the Swedish Parliament in December, 2008 commented that "Swedish family policies during the last 30 years have resulted in insecure children and youth, stressed adults and lower quality parenthood. As security in children is a strong social legacy, it is a negative spiral." Providing kindergarten and day-care "opportunities" for young children will do absolutely nothing to improve children's social skills, mental health or academic performance. What does make a difference is cultivating a context for the child to become attached to a parent, caregiver, teacher, educational assistant or child-care worker.

Attachment requires that the adult in the equation be willing and able to attend to and to protect the child; to help the child to feel that s/he is safe and accepted - no matter what. Providing the school system with more well-educated teachers is not the same as providing teachers who understand the developmental needs of their charges and who are willing to become emotionally involved with them. The law refers to educators as operating *in loco parentis*. Teachers need to be trained to be good "foster" parents while in school with our children.

Grade One Chaos

(This is a parent's story of the Neufeld paradigm in action. The story is complicated, especially when seen through the eyes of young child, but it is one that is repeatedly played out every year in many schools.)

Reluctant to return to school after a summer of family closeness, Sandy stood at the school door that first morning waiting to hear her name called. Passing the baton of attachment is not a ritual her school engages in because the belief is by Grade 1, children should be ready to take care of themselves. Hearing her name called by a woman she had never seen before, Sandy nervously hugged her mother, lined up in the Grade one "pen" behind children she was unfamiliar with, walked into a part of the school that was new to her and took her place at a desk as directed by the teacher. By the end of the first day, she left by the same door which she had arrived at six hours earlier; legs stiff, an untouched lunch, an expressionless face and little to say. After finding her tears with her mother, she shared that the day had been very eventful with rotations to music, physical activity and science but couldn't remember much about what actually happened during the day other than it was busy. Her mother, on seeing the young teacher saw fear in

the teacher's eyes and decided to connect with her the next day before school and again after school and she decided to make this ritual a daily mission.

Disappointed that her little friend from Kindergarten was in another class (there are three grade 1 classes at this school), Sandy's tears of futility came hard, fast and lengthy but by bedtime, she was ready to sleep peacefully, thinking about her teacher.
The third day of school, Sandy heard that if she read ten books, she would win a prize. That evening she couldn't get to sleep because she wanted to read all her books. After reading seven books, she decided to get up early to read another three and fill in her reading log. Certain that she would be acknowledged by her teacher for reading so many books, she left for school bubbling with enthusiasm. School dismissal was another lead-footed departure. She literally fell into her mother's arms, sobbing. Rubbing her back, kneeling on the playground, her intuitive mother softly said, "When I was a little girl, I decided to read because it felt good inside of me instead of reading for a prize". "But mommy" said Sandy, "I just want the teacher to like me".

At the close of the next day the teacher approached and took Sandy's hand saying "tomorrow is a new day and I look forward to seeing you". Lots of smiles, lots of warm gestures and a heavenly look came over Sandy's face. On the walk from school, her mother asked S what her teacher's first name was. In a deep, throaty, soft and passionate voice, she responded "Sally", "Sally Smith", "isn't that a beautiful name, mommy?" It was clear the relationship was beginning to form. Sandy now felt safe and that she liked the looks, sounds and experience of being in her teacher's presence.

The Ministry has guidelines: there are to be not more than 20 students per class. Sandy's class had 24 students. On the fifth day of school Sandy's parents received the dreaded phone call from the principal who had decided without consultation, that Sandy would be moved to a split grade one and two class at the beginning of the next week along with three other little girls who showed that their reading levels were above that of the other children. The principal explained that it would be presented to the girls in a favourable way which would illustrate that they were so smart that they had been chosen to move into a class where they would have special privileges. The new teacher would take them on a picnic the next week but for the time being they could stay in at recess to help their current teacher.

Sandy's parents weren't sure how to go about it but they were determined that their very sensitive, non-integrative and immature daughter was not moving to be with a teacher who had a reputation for expecting academic excellence (at any cost) from her students. They believed that Sandy was at the end of her resilience rope for now. They needed to tie the knot for her to hold on to. For the first time in her young life, Sandy was saying that she loved her teacher and loved school. Empathically, Sandy's mother shared her understanding of the predicament the principal had in following Ministry guidelines. The principal was informed that as parents, it was their decision that they wanted their daughter to stay with Mrs. Smith. Sandy was told that there would be some moving around of the students at school but mommy and daddy had decided she would stay with her current teacher. Sandy was told not to talk to anyone else about this because it might upset the other kids.

The principal, thinking that she might be able to sway Sandy's parents, decided to not share the conversation she had had with Sandy's parents. She did not tell the teacher that Sandy would *not* be moving. Mrs. Smith brought Sandy alongside her that next morning and explained that she *would* be moving into another class along with three of her classmates. Loyal to her parents, Sandy said nothing. When she was picked after school, Sandy said her day had been very frustrating because everyone said she was moving to another class but she knew she wasn't and she had to pretend to agree with what they were saying. Seemingly unphased (actually defended) she said, "I hope the adults figure this out soon". Reassuring her that it was up to the adults to make these decisions, she seemed to relax until her little brother came on the scene and she then started ordering him around and eventually punched him. Clearly, her alarm had dropped and her frustration erupted until her tsunamic tears came and finally left with three great gasps. All in the life of a little girl who just turned six years old.

Kids are away, teachers don't play

(Letter to the Editor Guelph Mercury, December 8, 2008)

As a speaker at the Wellington Catholic District School Board professional development day on Friday, December 5, I would like to thank both the Guelph Mercury and the School Board for seeing the pivotal position adults have in the lives of our most stuck kids. Until relatively recently, teachers were able to ride on the coattails of the strong adult orientations created and supported by culture and society. That was then, this is now. The problem we now face with regard to the education of our children is not something money can fix, curriculum can address nor technology remedy. The teachability of any particular student is the outcome of many factors.

As Brenda Kenyon said in her letter to the editor, a great deal can still be done to help children. Teachability requires a connection with the teacher, learning requires a relationship with a responsible adult whom the child looks up to, reaching full human potential requires a place in which a child can mature. Responsible adults have a powerful part to play in creating safe environments in which kids can thrive.

The Neufeld Paradigm and Knitting

While working with a 13 year old girl with no reliable attachments (a foster child who has been moved five times in the last year), it occurred to me that "knitting" might be an interesting approach to treatment.

Clearly, Hayley has very little resilience and is stuck in her frustration. With any unexpected changes or losses, she erupts in profanity, alienating anyone nearby. Hayley has no goals and is unable to consider the outcome of her actions. Her opinions rule and there is no room for misinterpretation nor another's point of view. Driven by her impulses Hayley's integrative capacity is blocked. She is unwilling to try anything new, she is easily bored and easily led by her peers. A wounded child (her parents abandoned her at age 8), Hayley carries the shame of rejection and the burden of society's expectations for perfection. Both her attention difficulties at school and her foul frustration led her to being expelled. In her defendedness, she claims that she doesn't care about school and refuses to attend.

Void of any healthy self-soothing techniques, Hayley does not have a relationship with herself and follows the lead of others without any passion. Recognizing that stability was required to anchor her energy, I became the compass point in her life for one hour a week.

My dilemma in using our time to address her adaptive, integrative and emergent needs opened the door to introducing knitting as a treatment approach.

Knitting taught her quickly that her dropped stitches weren't the end of the world. In fact, knitting showed her that managing her mistakes and not taking the mistakes or herself too seriously could be the bridge to looking at other parts of her life. Resilience started to unfold, integrative thinking came together and she began to feel pride in the outcome of her project. During the one hour of talking and knitting, Hayley did not lose her focus. My office is a shame-free zone, quiet and restful. She surrendered to me and I took the opportunity to use this dependence to transmit part of my culture to her. Hayley's face was relaxed but intent with no signs of alarm. She stayed under my direction without frustration nor self-attack.

As our time together evolved over several weeks, she talked about her Grandma knitting, her mother's difficulties and the pain about the loss of her family. She experienced no pressure from me to perform, to complete a perfect project, nor to have any form to her work.

I was able to draw out Hayley's desire to knit. I kept her safe and encouraged her to depend on me. I could script what was needed next. She was temporarily freed from her fears, from her preoccupations and from her woundedness.

Knitters navigate life's pain inside the shield of relationships, needles and yarn. Eventually, we need neither patterns nor directions. We celebrate originality before excellence, autonomy before correctness, meanings before manner and spirit before form.

School Start-up

In September, your child may be entering school or child-care. For some, this will be the beginning of another year. For others, this will be the first time they will experience a significant separation from their adult care-givers. For many of these children the experience will be - in a word - wounding. Woundedness results when an immature child is without a responsible adult to keep her safe.

Attachment acts as a shield around the child. It keeps him or her emotionally safe and makes it possible to withstand a variety of stresses: new settings, new peers, new regulations and new teachers. Without the shield of attachment the child is vulnerable and feels lost and insignificant.

Over the past several decades parents have been encouraged to push their children towards independence. "Attachment" has been seen as the basis for dependence and the argument has been made that dependence will somehow stunt the child's emotional growth. Actually, nothing could be further from the truth. As parents, we need to foster, not eliminate dependence. The more the child can safely depend on us, the safer their world feels. Our job should be to do everything possible to help our children to feel safe with responsible adults when we can't be around.

When our child enters school we have a perfect opportunity to bridge the gap from attachment at home to attachment in the classroom. We can provide something which will remind the child of us: a picture of our child and ourselves in a locket or wallet; a note tucked into a lunch box which reminds the child our love; an unexpected treat in the school bag. The specifics don't really matter. What matters is that we do something which reminds the child of his or her connection to us.

We can also make a point of passing "the baton of attachment". We can arrange to meet the teacher before school starts and we can demonstrate that we are comfortable and friendly with the teacher through eye contact, smiling and nodding to the teacher while our child watches. If we are safe and connected to the teacher, our child will feel comfortable.

We can also be watchful - both at home and at our child's school - for separation based discipline. "Time-outs" were designed for parents not children! When we use a time-out we are saying, "I don't want you around until you behave properly". Young children cannot make the link between their behaviour and whether or not they can remain emotionally safe with their parent or with their teacher. They ask, "Why should I trust this adult who without any reason that makes sense to me detaches from me - sends me away - leaves me alone and vulnerable?". Replace other alarm based discipline such as warnings, threat, intimidation, 1-2-3 magic with simple rules, structure and routine which will invite good behaviour and reduce feelings of separation.

The more time and effort we put into cultivating attachment with our children the greater their ability to cope with times when they must be away from us. Without a strong attachment even small challenges can become overwhelming; with attachment in place the child is able to develop more fully and completely.

Teachability and Kids

The Toronto Star reported on the research a Stanford University professor of psychology has conducted with Grade 5 pupils over a period of 10 years. She found that those who were praised for their hard work performed better than those praised for their intelligence. From this research her yearning was for, "parents and educators to transform their view of intelligence from something children have to something we can help them cultivate".

When teachers have the stance that intelligence is something students can develop through their own efforts and education, students become excited about taking on challenges, because that will lead to learning. If success is the result of just being smart then students will avoid tasks that might reveal their deficiencies.

This research is another example of how mind-set influences a child's ability to be taught. There is much more that we can do to help our children reach their full learning potential. The learning equation is further enhanced when we understand what it is that renders a child teachable.

Dr. Gordon Neufeld states, "There is no doubt that attachment is the most powerful motivating force of all but it must be harnessed to be used for teaching purposes. Unless we win the hearts of our children, we are unlikely to have much influence on their minds".

Within a learning context like school or childcare, attachment can be primed by using our instincts to greet each child warmly by name. Collecting their eyes, inviting a smile and a nod is something that we work very hard at doing whenever a baby is in our presence. When a baby takes our finger, we feel the connection. Children of all ages yearn for this kind of connection. With older children we can provide something other than a finger to hold on to by showing our delight and interest in their presence. Praise does not have the same lasting effect as connection does because it is conditional upon performance. Inviting children to exist in our presence with warmth, enjoyment and delight goes much further.

Adults must have the alpha position with children. We must always act as a child's compass point and assume the responsibility to orient the child, especially in times of confusion and disorientation. Encouraging the child to depend on the adult in charge can be done by reaching out to the child and reassuring him/her that eventually she will be able to do what she is trying to do and that s/he will get there. Actively arranging situations where the child will need to depend on you fosters the context in which the child feels safe and in a position to try something new.

When dealing with the immature, we need to win their hearts to open their minds to our influence.

A Little Theory

"When I work with attachment issues the most important feature of the therapy is to provide a safe, secure environment in which the client feels truly heard."

Attachment

In my work with both children and adults I have found that many of their personal and relationship problems can be traced to the kind of attachment which they have to others. In many cases people have had a childhood or experiences as they grew up in which they were not able to form trusting, safe relationships with others. Many times, this results in difficulty in forming close, stable relationships such as marriage or even close, long-lasting friendships.

When I work with attachment issues the most important feature of the therapy is to provide a safe, secure environment in which the client feels truly heard. Many clients will find it difficult to trust the fact that they can talk openly about their fears, their desires and their hopes and that they will not be rejected or judged. I encourage clients to examine their past relationships and the relationships which they have around them in the present and to explore these - to experiment - and see what their concerns are as they attempt to form more stable trusting relationships that are meaningful and satisfying.

There is a huge literature available if you want to study this field. Some of the most recent writing deals with the ways in which the infant's brain is actually affected by the kind of attention and caring which it receives from the adults (usually the mother) who raise it. This is an exciting branch of neuroscience - the new frontier which unites psychology, neurology and those who study the chemistry of the brain.

Why Kids Need Strong Attachments with the Adults who are Responsible for Them

Attachment is an instinctual drive that is found in all forms of life. For children, it is the most important need, even more important than hunger. Babies have to be attached before they can be fed.

Attachment is the context for raising children. It is like the umbilical cord that keeps the child attached to the responsible adults in his/her life and it has a force which creates the closeness necessary so that the child feels connected, valued and special. Attachment allows for dependence. It provides the energy to keep adults in a place of feeling responsible to move any road blocks out of the way of the child's natural development.

When attachment needs are sufficiently met, young children are ready to emerge as individuals but only for very short periods of time. This means that if the parents are in the same room with the child and the child is feeling fulfilled (sufficiently attached), the child may spontaneously start to play with his toys or create a picture by himself without any direction. This process is called emergent play and it is the beginning of creativity.

For adolescents this time of preparing for emergence as an individual is more intense. In this time of vulnerability, adolescents naturally become morose or melancholic, wanting to be alone more often to carefully consider: their own thoughts and feelings and who they are in relationship with the world and with others. During this time of withdrawal, parents often work hard at trying to make their adolescent cheer up rather than reassuring them that this time of sadness is a natural part of the process of growing up.

Becoming an individual with her own thoughts, feelings, and opinions grows from this place of sadness or grief. Once personal individuality is accepted, adolescents or young adults are then able to experience their separateness from the individuality of others. Integrating into society without the loss of self is maturation and it inevitably takes many years to accomplish. It is done best within the context of attachment to those adults who are responsible for the growth and development of the young person.

Children and adolescents need to be attached to parents, grand-parents, child-care providers, and teachers. At present we are pushing our children to integrate into society before they have roots of attachment and before they have reached the developmental stage in which they can be both separate and together with others.

Social development cannot be forced by having children relate to children; in fact, it can wither. Children need to have strong attachments with adults who are responsible for them so that they can rest in the natural evolution of development.

Parents are responsible for their relationships with children.

A Short Bibliography on Attachment

Bowlby, J. (1988). A secure base. Clinical application of attachment theory. London: Routledge.

Damasio (1998) Emotion in the perspective of the integrated nervous system. *Brain Research Reviews, 26,* 83-86.

Greenspan, S.I., & Wieder, S. (2006). Engaging autism: Using the floortime approach to help children relate, communicate and think. New Hork: Perseus.

Karen, R. (1998). Becoming attached: First relationships and how they shape our capacity to love. Oxford University Press.

Neufeld, G. (2013). Hold on to Your Kids. Toronto: Random House (2nd ed.).

Schore, D. (2001). Effects of a secure attachment relationship on right brain development, affect regulation, and infant mental health. *Infant Mental Health Journal, 22,* 7-66.

Schore, D. (2012). The science of the art of psychotherapy. Toronto: W.W. Norton & Co.

Siegel, D. (199). The developing mind: How relationships and the brain interact to shape who we are. New York: Guilford.

Questing for Value

Across the lifespan, change comes from developing our relational capacities rather than learning specific techniques related to behaviour. Were it not for the peculiar combination of being able to both read in another what is being felt and being able to intuit what another is thinking, we would not have evolved to be humans. By the fourth year of life, children have figured out that Mommy and Daddy hold close what they hold dear. Dr. Gordon Neufeld, a Vancouver-based developmental psychologist points out that there are attachment roots that represent ways to hold close those who matter.

The first two roots of attachment grow quickly to satisfy both our sensory needs and our desire to identify with or to be the same as others. Deeper than conformity and sameness, is the need to satiate a sense of being able to carry the essence of another's closeness within. One evening while rubbing my grand-daughter's back as she fell asleep she quietly shared , in a deeply relaxed voice, "You know grandma, I can feel your hand on my back when you aren't touching me and I can even feel it there when you aren't here". She was now able to carry me within her, feeling that she belonged to me and I to her. She was at rest and drifted into slumber.

Both children and adults hunger to belong, to have value, to have influence and to measure up to the expectations of others. We alter our appearance, search for flaws in ourselves and others, become preoccupied with materialism and reach for perfection, all in an effort to win approval and to feel the warmth of an invitation to spend time on committees, to belong to an organization and to be part of a community.

What happens when there is no room for us to exist in the presence of others; when there is no one to take our side; no one to help keep us out of trouble or to stand up for us when we least expect it, and at the same time insinuate, "you're not as good as you think you are."? We feel the rejection, the deep shame, the put-down hidden inside of what passes for humour and the humiliation of feeling we are not good enough. These disloyalties rip us apart and we are left defending ourselves by withdrawing or hardening our hearts in order to survive.
To matter is the essence of life.

Searching for golden nuggets from others as rewards for our achievements is a way of working to close the gap between ourselves and how others see us. We want to influence the verdict of others. Trying to win approval by reaching for perfection cheats us in our quest for value. We not only become insecure and insatiable but we also close the door to true intimacy. We yearn to have another truly know us and with that understanding of being known inside-out, the deepest capacity for relationship fulfillment is achieved. Our value is reflected in the eyes of others. This mirror effect combined with the capacity to put ourselves emotionally and cognitively in someone else's shoes – regardless of their age - to feel what they feel and to be interested in them is the window into another's world. Relationships are about satisfying the quest for value by giving invitations to exist, by making room for another to matter, and by making certain that people of all ages feel at home in our presence.

Heloise

Last evening, my husband, David's one-woman play "Heloise" was read by an award-winning, professional actor Colleen Williams at the Unitarian Church in Guelph. The play tells of the tragic 12th century love affair between Peter Abelard, Europe's most respected philosopher and teacher, and the brilliantly gifted young woman Heloise, and its tragic outcome.
I couldn't believe my ears as I heard the unfolding of Heloise's description of the roots of attachment she had developed with her Abelard. Her initial attraction to him was of course sensory. Through intellect, drawing out their similarities and her significance to him, he masterfully satisfied her young sensuous spirit and moved all impediments out of the way of taking her virginity. As lovers, Abelard and Heloise secretly luxuriated in a passionate relationship under the eaves of her uncle's roof until she was obviously with child. Abelard, dressed her in nun's robes and sent her to a nunnery by horse and barge many miles away.

Heloise delivered their son, Astrolabe, under great stress; alone, frightened and distraught. She remained loyal to Abelard begging him to allow himself to get to know her inside –out. He demanded she marry him, insisted on keeping their marriage secret (he was a teacher who had sinned) and tried to convince her through his "ethics of intention" that they could exist together. Eventually, they were discovered by Heloise's guardian. Abelard was castrated, healed, dedicated his life to the church and Heloise became the abbess of the convent where she had sought refuge. In the second act, Heloise standing at Abelard's coffin with the letters she had written to him during their estrangement, pounded on his coffin in tears. Her tears of frustration changed to tears of futility. At that pivotal moment, she shared with the audience that Abelard was a vulnerable man who could not bear the burden of his jealousy. His fear that he would lose her to another man drove him away from any closeness.

Heloise connected through her senses and yearned for Abelard to both know and value her intimately. He just couldn't get past the "belonging to him" root. Heloise stayed loyal to her man, lived out her life as the leader of the convent but in her heart worshipped not God, but Abelard.
I think David's exposure to the paradigm, without his awareness, has cultivated a place inside of him that has given him a voice of "the heart". Evidence of spirit graced with some form. A good read which is available on request.

Appendices

Appendix A : A profile of Ben

After meeting Ben in my office for the first time, my sense of alarm and urgency was greatly reduced. It is clear to me now that I was strongly influenced by the horrifying newspaper report regarding him and the implications of gun carrying youth in our school culture.

Attachment

Ben is strongly attached to his peer group and the excitement of their pursuits. He has attached through his senses; through a feeling of belonging; by being loyal to the same values, and by developing a sense of importance within the context of his group. His mother describes him as having been extremely attached to his nanny and in the past whenever he had difficulty with the limits at school, the nanny dealt with the consequences. Ben has been to private school, an alternative school, a camp for troubled kids and now in a public school in a city where is mother would like to have a fresh start without his nanny. Within each system Ben has found a peer group to which he felt polarized and in which there was a built-in frame of reference.

Alarm and Attachment

Since his toddler years, Ben has been detached from his parents. Each year he has increased his detachment from traditional society, now backing out of possible relationships with teachers, classes at school, a part-time job, and school culture as a whole. He spends his time "chilling out" with his friends, smoking and drinking beer wherever, whenever and with whomever he can connect. He has no life goals other than to live out his values which are "anti-establishment". He will not acquire any credits this year for Grade 10. His high state of alarm is evident as he sits in the chair: searching for his lighter which he flicks for emphasis; pulling his pubic hairs out through the fly of his shorts which are placed six inches above the belt of his pants and picking a scab on his arm.

Ben is attached to money and to things. Most of his violent arguments with his parents are about the flow of money and clothes that he wishes to purchased. For the most part they have acquiesced.

Ben dresses in 'gangsta' style clothes. His tastes are very much a part of the culture with choices that look expensive. He is a big boy - over six feet tall - who has been provided with access to ample food and drink.

Ben's only sibling who is eight years his senior has had a trouble-free growing-up, earned a university education and now travels the world as a public speaker for an international children's organization. They see little of each other but according to Ben have a respectful relationship (his brother doesn't minimize his values).

Maturation

Ben's adaptive functioning is compromised. His mother readily admits until she became involved in a parent support group, Ben had very few "no's" to contend with and for the most part has had his own way. There has been no invitation to his sadness from anyone.

Ben does not question his own decisions. Like his mother, he stands behind what he says and does. He expresses no regrets about the state of his life and is highly motivated to live the values defined by his peer group. Integrative functioning was somewhat apparent when he started to think about how to finance his cigarette habit. He thought on the one hand he could steal to pay for his cigarettes and on the other hand he could find a job as a dishwasher. He also demonstrated his mix by choosing to use a pellet gun rather than a real one for his run through the school.

For many years Ben's bias to individuate from his parents has been strong. He seems to be clear that there is no room for him in the relationship with his parents should he make

different choices than they would. His emergent functioning is strong but only to the point where he wants to be the polar opposite to his parents, especially his mother.

Vulnerability

Ben's predisposition to sensitivity is most likely both genetic and contextual. His defended (red-headed) father, full of foul frustration refused to meet conjointly with his ex-wife. A great deal of acrimony exists between the two parents.

Ben speaks of his nanny in a soft-voice as he explains that she is the only person who really understood him. The loss of her shield must be unbearable for him. Without attachments both at school and at home he is masking his woundedness by appearing uncaring. I would think that in his extreme alarm state he was attracted to the group in which he felt a sense of belonging.

Ben explained that in his early years, the chaos in his home was overwhelming. A discussion with his mother is so "over stimulating" that he has to "dump profanity all over her" and search out his friends so he can "chill out".

Final comment

My thinking is that his mother moves in too quickly with her arguments, feminist values and demands which drive his brain to protect his vulnerability and he runs. Ben seeks solace in his friends, his cigarettes, his beer and edgy criminal activities and probably his use of marijuana will be uncovered in the future.

Appendix B: A Developmental 3D Analysis – Annie

(The material in this analysis was prepared to assist students completing their Directed Studies Program for the Neufeld Institute training progam.)

Presenting Concern

Annie is 15 years old and has three older siblings. Her parents contacted me via e-mail explaining that Annie had never "bonded" to the family constellation. They described Annie as destructive, aggressive, bossy, rough and "deliberately" disobedient. At school, she was aloof and did not engage in social interaction or classroom activities.

Recently, she had been suspended from school for non-attendance and had retreated to her bed for a month. Annie always wanted her own way with her life, ordering her parents to meet her demands and erupting with frustration when they did not comply. Withdrawn from her family after destroying $8000 worth of computer equipment at her school, her parents moved her into a home supported by their church to provide respite for themselves. The goal of this placement was to keep her safe and to help her to come to a place of remorse concerning her recent behaviour.

History and Context

Annie is dark-skinned, born to a single white mother who, at age 17 had a relationship with a black man while she was on vacation in Bermuda. Annie was raised in her grandparents' home on a farm in northern Ontario until she was three years old. She then lived with her mother in a very small apartment in a city close to the farm. Annie's mother was depressed and soon became involved a culture of drugs and alcohol. During her early years, Annie was responsible for both her own personal care as well that of her mother (who was seldom present either physically or emotionally).

At the age of 8 while she was at a babysitter's, her mother was killed in a head-on collision. Family and Children's Services intervened and Annie was placed with her maternal uncle (Paul) and his family 200 km. from her grandparents' home. In the beginning, she was a shy, sweet, quiet, "good" girl, who did as she was told.

By age 10, Annie's aggression came out through tantrums, foul name-calling and destroying anything breakable. Her adoptive mother and father handled her aggression with consequences, time-outs, hours of discussion and threats. As fundamentalists, her parents were horrified at her outbursts and her language. Finding Annie too hard to handle, mother would often cry in helplessness and beg her to be better behaved. Her father prayed for

Annie and remained optimistic that God would intervene and that Annie "would come to her senses". Her siblings no longer interacted with her.

Snapshot

Annie has great difficulty forming relationships with anyone. She is constantly finding ways to avoid being with people at school, at home and at church. At times she is quiet and aloof and then without much warning, she becomes "possessed". Annie tells her mother what to do, is embarrassed by her mother's clothes, and criticizes her "weaknesses" and her "inability" to work outside the home. Annie will not receive care from anyone and makes fun of her sensitive 18 year old brother (who is home-schooled) and her 23 year old developmentally disabled sister. She longs for contact with her married older sister who is a teacher in Halifax. Annie takes charge of conversations when she is alone with her mother and ignores her father. She does not listen to her parents and will resist their direction. She runs away from home, walked away from her job at a fast food restaurant and left her school without permission. Her behaviour in the home is destructive, wild and brazen. Consequences and time-outs have never worked with her. At one point, as a result of having possessions taken away as a negative consequence she had only her bed left in her room. Her meals were left outside her door and she ate sparingly. Her parents would try to show her what couldn't and wouldn't work but she would plug her ears and roll over if they came to her room. Her behaviour is untempered in all contexts. She is either in "shut down" mode or violently throwing and smashing breakables. Her parents and siblings are afraid of her and offer no warmth, complaining that she has no conscience.

Developmental 3D Analysis
Attachment

Born seven weeks too soon by Caesarian section, Annie was described by her adoptive parents as having been a very fussy baby and difficult toddler who did not "bond" with her mother nor anyone else during the eight years they had together. Annie is highly sensitive and has experienced overwhelming *wounds* throughout her short life. On meeting her for the first time, I noticed that her face was flat, her pupils were dilated and she was unable to hold my gaze.

Most of her energy in the past two years (since her initiation to high school) has been consumed by trying to hide from the world. She is not ready to be in a large school with a multitude of teachers and no anchors. She stayed in her bed and was suspended from school for non-attendance. Since living with the respite family, she has returned to a different school in a new area of town and is one of ten students in a special make-up class. Until recently, Annie has cut herself off from the world around her, not trusting that those responsible for her could keep her safe. Annie has tried to look after herself.

When she was living with her adoptive parents Janice and Paul, she thwarted their requests and became increasingly destructive. She would lie, steal and break their possessions when things didn't go her way. Her adoptive father explained that this was her pattern her whole life including the time with her biological mother. Both Janice and Paul believed that "once Annie was in their home, having a consistent family life that she would feel gratitude and heal".

I spoke with Hilary, the family matriarch in Annie's respite home. Hilary described Annie as hard-working, never still, always wanting to anticipate what they might want or need as well as doing whatever they asked of her. Constantly trying to please, Annie became very attached to hard work and refuses any gestures that might resemble someone caring for her. She does not have a relationship with anyone including herself. Annie is a lost child without any anchors. She has no passion, no curiosity, no interests and no vitality. Annie is a *stuck* child who was emotionally and physically abandoned by her biological parents and emotionally abandoned by her adoptive parents.

Without the shield of safe emotional relationships with responsible adults, Annie has nowhere to cry, and nowhere to grieve all that has not gone her way.

Vulnerability

Annie's vulnerability is pervasive and manifests itself through her empty gaze and expressionless face. Relationships have proven to be too painful to bear for Annie. The automatic drive in her brain which protects her from pain is in overdrive. The unblinking blankness in Annie's eyes indicates that she has numbed out, tuned out and backed out of both relationships and the world around her. Full of alarm, her foul frustration erupts and as Annie describes it, "my brain leaves my head and I lose control". Unable to talk about what frustrates her, Annie does not cry. Janice, her adoptive mother, has never seen her have her tears over anything that has hurt her emotionally or physically. Both her experience and expression of frustration are untempered.

Predisposed to sensitivity, Annie has also endured multiple traumas throughout her short life. Annie is the only person in her fundamentalist church who has dark skin. In a state of defensive detachment, Annie's counterwill is engaged when her adoptive parents ask her to do anything. However, while living with the respite family, she is driven to please. Annie's obsessive robotic need to please the respite family is an indication that her alarm is high and that she has created a new outlet for her frustration. Along with finger picking that has developed while in the respite home, Annie's restlessness is on the rise.

My sense is that Annie's counterwill is primarily fuelled by her adoptive parents' expectation that she be grateful for their generosity in bringing her into their family. Annie sense that she is being coerced or manipulated pushes her into defensive detachment. Annie distrusts any feeling of dependency. The brew of deep attachment wounds, predisposed sensitivities, early childhood trauma, the rigidity of a very strict religious community and adoptive parents who are afraid of being wrong has provoked all the defenses that this young woman possesses.

Maturation

Emergent Functioning

Annie's *emergent functioning* is compromised. Annie's innate desire for self-mastery is somewhat apparent in her drive to look after herself and others in the respite home yet while in her adoptive home she took to her bed to hide from the world. On the one hand Annie looks on the surface as though she is independent. Looking a little deeper, it is clear that she has no sense of herself and caters to those in her respite family home. On the other hand, when with her adoptive family, Annie retreats to her bed to escape the confusion she is experiencing about who she is and where she fits. In both cases she is fleeing dependency from all adults.

Adaptive Functioning

Annie has no capacity for *adapting* to all that has not worked for her. Her adoptive mother Mary believes that tears are a sign of weakness and has never understood the importance of priming *adaptive functioning* as a responsibility of parenting. Believing that "sacrificing" herself for her children has left Janice full of frustration too.

Annie has seven years of grief which needs to be addressed, beginning with the tragic loss of her biological mother. She has not adapted to "standing out" as different by having dark skin in a white culture. Annie's attachment hunger is adding to her frustration. Currently, there is no one to lead her out of her stuckness, no one who is resourceful and resilient who can walk beside her through all the losses, all the confusion, and all the disappointments which she has experienced in her life.

3D ANALYSIS: Snapshot highlights
Pursuit of Proximity

Annie has great difficulty forming relationships with anyone. She is constantly finding ways to avoid being with people at school, at home and at church. At times she is quiet and aloof and then without much warning, she becomes "possessed". Annie tells her mother what to do, is embarrassed by her mother's clothes, criticizes her "weaknesses" and her "inability" to work outside the home. Annie will not receive care from anyone and makes fun of her sensitive 18 year old adoptive brother (who is home-schooled) and her 23 year old developmentally disabled sister. She longs for contact with her married older sister who is a teacher in Halifax. Annie takes charge of conversations when she is alone with her mother and ignores her father. She does not listen to her parents and will resist their direction. She runs away from home, walked away from her job at a fast-food restaurant and left her school without permission. Her behaviour in the home is destructive, wild and brazen. Consequences and time-outs have never worked for her. At one point, all she had left in her room was her bed. Her meals were left outside her door and she ate sparingly. Her parents would try to show her what couldn't and wouldn't work but she would plug her ears and roll over if they came to her room. Her behaviour is untempered in all contexts. She is either in "shut down" mode or violently throwing and smashing breakables. Her parents and siblings are afraid of her and offer no warmth complaining that she has no conscience.

Comments: Annie is missing a functional attachment with a responsible adult. Abandoned by her biological father after conception and losing her biological mother in a car accident, she has not experienced an invitation to exist in the presence of a warm, caring adult who can shield her from the expectations of society. Annie requires rest, warmth, nurturing, room to grow and a safe emotional relationship in which her heart can soften. Inside the womb of right relationship, Annie will find her tears, and the dam will break to unleash all the pent up toxicity that has held back nature's master plan from unfolding as it should.

Defenses Against Vulnerability

Annie has great difficulty forming relationships with anyone. She is constantly finding ways to avoid being with people at school, at home and at church. At times she is quiet and aloof and then without much warning, she becomes "possessed". Annie tells her mother what to do, is embarrassed by her mother's clothes, criticizes her "weaknesses" and her "inability" to work outside the home. Annie will not receive care from anyone and makes fun of her sensitive 18 year old adoptive brother (who is home-schooled) and her 23 year old *developmentally disabled sister. She longs for contact with her married older sister who is a teacher in Halifax. Annie takes charge of conversations when she is alone with her mother and ignores her father. She does not listen to her parents and will resist their direction. She runs away from home, walked away from her job at a fast food restaurant and left her school without permission. Her behaviour in the home is destructive, wild and brazen. Consequences and time-outs have never worked for her. At one point, all she had left in her room was her bed. Her meals were left outside her door and she ate sparingly. Her parents would try to show her what couldn't and wouldn't work but she would plug her ears and roll over if they came to her room. Her behaviour is untempered in all contexts. She is either in "shut down" mode or violently throwing and smashing breakables. Her parents and siblings are afraid of her and offer no warmth complaining that she has no conscience.*

Comments: Highly sensitive from conception, Annie has experienced more losses than most people do in a lifetime. Unable to handle her painful situation, Annie became stuck in defending her vulnerability. As a result of her energy being consumed with defending herself, Annie's emotional and developmental growth has become compromised. She has been pushed into taking the Alpha position since age three. Instinctively she has resisted contact and closeness, fearing further wounds of separation. During the last year, feeling more and more pressure to honour her parents' values, Annie's defense mechanisms are on high alert (*defensive detachment*). The context for both healthy development and parenting has been destroyed.

Lack of Adaptive Functioning

Annie has great difficulty forming relationships with anyone. She is constantly finding ways to avoid being with people at school, at home and at church. At times she is quiet and aloof and then without much warning, she becomes "possessed". Annie tells her mother what to do, is embarrassed by her mother's clothes, criticizes her "weaknesses" and her "inability" to work outside the home. Annie will not receive care from anyone and makes fun of her sensitive 18 year old adoptive brother (who is home-schooled) and her 23 year old developmentally disabled sister. She longs for contact with her married older sister who is a teacher in Halifax. Annie takes charge of conversations when she is alone with her mother and ignores her father. She does not listen to her parents and will resist their direction. She runs away from home, walked away from her job at a fast food restaurant and left her school without permission. Her behaviour in the home is destructive, wild and brazen. _Consequences and time-outs have never worked for her._ At one point, all she had left in her room was her bed. Her meals were left outside her door and she ate sparingly. Her parents would try to _show her what couldn't and wouldn't work but_ she would plug her ears and roll over if they came to her room. Her behaviour is untempered in all contexts. She is either in _"shut down"_ mode or violently throwing and smashing breakables. Her parents and siblings are afraid of her and offer no warmth complaining that she has no conscience.

Comments: Annie is stuck in trying to resist those who are in charge. Consequently, she has not developed resilience to handle activities of daily life. Feeling overwhelmed with her school and home situation and with nowhere to put her feelings Annie retreated to her room. She refused to come out, ate her meals in isolation and only left her room if there was no one else in the house. During this time she did little more than sleep, keeping herself warm under many layers of blankets. She did have some suicidal ideation at this time.

Lack of Integrative Functioning

Annie has great _difficulty forming relationships with anyone._ She is constantly finding _ways to avoid being with people at school, at home and at church._ At times she is quiet and aloof and then without much warning, she becomes "possessed". Annie tells her mother what to do, is embarrassed by her mother's clothes, criticizes her "weaknesses" and her "inability" to work outside the home. Annie will not receive care from anyone _and makes fun of her sensitive 18 year old adoptive brother (who is home-schooled) and her 23 year old developmentally disabled sister._ She longs for contact with her married older sister who is a teacher in Halifax. Annie takes charge of conversations when she is alone with her mother and ignores her father. She _does not listen to her parents and will resist their direction._ She runs away from home, walked away from her job at a fast food restaurant and left her school without permission. Her behaviour in the home is destructive, wild and brazen. Consequences and time-outs have never worked for her. At one point, all she had left in her room was her bed. Her meals were left outside her door and she ate sparingly. _Her parents would try to show her what couldn't and wouldn't work but she would plug her ears and roll over if they came to her room. Her behaviour is _untempered_ in all contexts. She is either in "shut down" mode or violently throwing and smashing breakables. Her parents and siblings are afraid of her and offer no warmth complaining that she has <u>no conscience</u>.

Comments: Driven by her instincts and unable to feel the ambivalence between impulse and intentions, Annie's aggression is untempered, she lacks a conscience and is unable to sort out what is working and what isn't working for her.

Common Core Issues and Dynamics

Aggression

Annie has great difficulty forming relationships with anyone. She is constantly finding ways to avoid being with people at school, at home and at church. At times she is quiet and aloof and then without much warning, she becomes "possessed". Annie tells her mother what to do, is embarrassed by her mother's clothes, criticizes her "weaknesses" and her "inability" to work outside the home. Annie will not receive care from anyone and makes fun of her sensitive 18 year old adoptive brother (who is home-schooled) and her 23 year old developmentally disabled sister. She longs for contact with her married older sister who is a teacher in Halifax. Annie takes charge of conversations when she is alone with her mother and ignores her father. She does not listen to her parents and will resist their direction. She runs away from home, walked away from her job at a fast food restaurant and left her school

without permission. <u>Her behaviour in the home is destructive, wild and brazen.</u> Consequences and time-outs have never worked for her. At one point, all she had left in her room was her bed. Her meals were left outside her door and she ate sparingly. <u>Her parents would try to show her what couldn't and wouldn't work but she would plug her ears and roll over if they came to her room. Her behaviour is untempered in all contexts.</u> She is either in "shut down" mode or <u>violently throwing and smashing breakables.</u> Her parents and siblings are afraid of her and offer no warmth complaining that she has no conscience.

Comments: Annie was told it was school policy that because of her absenteeism she could not return to the school in which she was enrolled. Annie's foul frustration became aggression and she destroyed $8000 worth of computer equipment with her bare hands, leaving her parents frightened and concerned.

Annie felt no remorse over this incident but was dry-eyed. Her mother explained that it is rare for Annie to show any emotion other than frustration and disgust. Because Annie is defended against vulnerability and unable to feel the futility of things not going her way, her foul frustration turns into a relentless attack. Her dry eyes reflect how stuck she is in the adaptive process.

Alarm

Annie has great difficulty forming relationships with anyone. She is constantly finding ways to avoid being with people at school, at home and at church. At times she is quiet and aloof and then without much warning, she becomes "possessed". Annie tells her mother what to do, is embarrassed by her mother's clothes, criticizes her "weaknesses" and her "inability" to work outside the home. Annie will not receive care from anyone and makes fun of her sensitive 18 year old adoptive brother (who is home-schooled) and her 23 year old developmentally disabled sister. She longs for contact with her married older sister who is a teacher in Halifax. Annie takes charge of conversations when she is alone with her mother and ignores her father. She does not listen to her parents and will resist their direction. She runs away from home, walked away from her job at a fast food restaurant and left her school without permission. Her behaviour in the home is destructive, wild and brazen. Consequences and time-outs have never worked for her. At one point, all she had left in her room was her bed. Her meals were left outside her door and she ate sparingly. Her parents would try to show her what couldn't and wouldn't work but she would plug her ears and roll over if they came to her room. Her behaviour is untempered in all contexts. She is either in "shut down" mode or violently throwing and smashing breakables. Her parents and siblings are afraid of her and offer no warmth complaining that she has no conscience.

Comments: In Annie's attempts to "be good" she channels the alarm she feels into her finger picking habit which draws blood. She spends long periods of time trimming the broken edges of her nails with clippers and scissors. Clearly agitated when sitting with me, she revealed that 80% of the time she experiences the need (the compulsion) to either pick or manicure the edges of her nails. Like cutting, this act of picking until drawing blood increases the adrenalin in her body. It may be another way to elevate dopamine levels when they become low due to her depression.

Annie does not feel safe in relationships with responsible adults. The closer she becomes the more she fears separation. Feelings of not mattering are often evoked in Annie and trigger her underlying neuroses. It seems that Annie's parents are unable to invite some parts of her to exist. I am thinking these parts are those which they cannot invite to exist within themselves.

Annie has become obsessed with "doing the job right". Two weeks ago, she spent ten consecutive hours pulling weeds from her respite family's lawn. Preparing food must be perfect and she involves herself in long hours of planning, cooking and executing the meals for both families. Her attachment hunger for relationships may be fulfilled with her preoccupation with food preparation.

Separation

Annie has great difficulty forming relationships with anyone. She is constantly finding ways to avoid being with people at school, at home and at church. At times she is quiet and aloof and then without much warning, she becomes "possessed". Annie tells her mother what to do, is embarrassed by her mother's clothes, criticizes her "weaknesses" and her "inability" to work outside the home. *Annie will not receive care from anyone* and makes fun of her sensitive 18 year old adoptive brother (who is home-schooled) and her 23 year old developmentally disabled sister. *She longs for contact with her married older sister who is a teacher in Halifax.* Annie takes charge of conversations when she is alone with her mother and ignores her father. She does not listen to her parents and will resist their direction. She runs away from home, walked away from her job at a fast food restaurant and left her school without permission. Her behaviour in the home is destructive, wild and*

brazen. Consequences and time-outs have never worked for her. At one point, all she had left in her room was her bed. Her meals were left outside her door and she ate sparingly. Her parents would try to show her what couldn't and wouldn't work but she would plug her ears and roll over if they came to her room. Her behaviour is untempered in all contexts. She is either in "shut down" mode or violently throwing and smashing breakables. Her parents and siblings are afraid of her and offer no warmth complaining that she has no conscience.*

Annie has experienced many psychological and emotional losses. Her move to another home (competing attachments) and the threat that if she doesn't change she could become a foster child has triggered all of her attachment wounds. The loss of her biological mother, the abandonment by her biological father, the loss of her maternal grandmother, the loss of her place with her friends and her school prior to high school give her brain no option but to protect and defend. She does not feel emotionally understood by anyone. Both the emphasis on behaviour and invoking "God's punishment" when she doesn't comply have left little room for relationship. Much of Annie's alarm, domination, foul frustration and defended detachment are apparent in her experience of anxiety in relationships.

Dominance

Annie has great difficulty forming relationships with anyone. She is constantly finding ways to avoid being with people at school, at home and at church. At times she is quiet and aloof and then without much warning, she becomes "possessed". Annie tells her mother what to do, is embarrassed by her mother's clothes, criticizes her "weaknesses" and her "inability" to work outside the home. Annie will not receive care from anyone and makes fun of her sensitive 18 year old adoptive brother (who is home-schooled) and her 23 year old developmentally disabled sister. She longs for contact with her married older sister who is a teacher in Halifax. Annie takes charge of conversations when she is alone with her mother and ignores her father. She does not listen to her parents and will resist their direction. She runs away from home, walked away from her job at a fast food restaurant and left her school without permission. Her behaviour in the home is destructive, wild and brazen. Consequences and time-outs have never worked for her. At one point, all she had left in her room was her bed. Her meals were left outside her door and she ate sparingly. Her parents would try to show her what couldn't and wouldn't work but she would plug her ears and roll over if

they came to her room. Her behaviour is untempered in all contexts. She is either in "shut down" mode or violently throwing and smashing breakables. Her parents and siblings are afraid of her and offer no warmth complaining that she has no conscience.

Comment: Taking on the Alpha position in the respite family home is being further exacerbated by the transitioning agenda (moving Annie back to her adoptive parents' home) created by the church counsellor. Annie is required to cook (from scratch) and host a dinner for her parents prepared only by her in an attempt to woo them back into relationship with her. This is to be held once a week for a month in the respite family home. Annie has only known attachment by being in the dominant position, first with her unhealthy biological mother, then with her adoptive family and now with her respite family. Insecurely attached and emotionally unsafe, Annie has no compass and no anchors.

In many ways, Annie feels controlled and can find no rest. Family life in both homes and the church provide rigid structure with no room for Annie to find her own footing and venture forth. She is yearning to have an adult find a place which will provide rest for her so that she can abandon taking care of herself.

Counterwill

Annie has great difficulty forming relationships with anyone. She is constantly <u>finding ways to avoid being with people at school, at home and at church</u>. At times she is quiet and aloof and then without much warning, she becomes "possessed". Annie tells her mother what to do, is embarrassed by her mother's clothes, criticizes her "weaknesses" and her "inability" to work outside the home. Annie will not receive care from anyone and makes fun of her sensitive 18 year old adoptive brother (who is home-schooled) and her 23 year old developmentally disabled sister. She longs for contact with her married older sister who is a teacher in Halifax. Annie takes charge of conversations when she is alone with her mother and ignores her father. <u>She does not listen to her parents and will resist their direction.</u> She runs away from home, walked away from her job at a fast food restaurant and left her school without permission. Her behaviour in the home is destructive, wild and brazen. Consequences and time-outs have never worked for her. At one point, all she had left in her room was her bed. Her meals were left outside her door and she ate sparingly. Her parents would try to show her what couldn't and wouldn't work but <u>she would plug her ears and roll over if they came to her room.</u> Her behaviour

is untempered in all contexts. She is either in "shut down" mode or violently throwing and smashing breakables. Her parents and siblings are afraid of her and offer no warmth complaining that she has no conscience.

Comment: Annie's counterwill problems are chronic. Annie feels coerced and controlled by both of her parents as well as by the church. Pressured to fit into the values which the family holds dear (no telephone after 10:00 p.m., no more than ten minutes on the computer per day, work hard, pay your own way and contribute with the intention to benefit all others), Annie reacts by rolling her eyes and minimizing any suggestions from her parents. She shows absolutely no interest in family activities. For the most part, Annie has no motivation to do anything. Sullenness overtakes her and she often locks herself in her room for many days at a time *(emotional counterwill)*. She senses when her parents have agendas for her and her instincts drive her to thwart their expectations and send her fleeing to her bedroom, refusing to get out of bed for days Her refusal to go to school targets another family value which is equal in importance to the Church *(psychological counterwill)*. Fulfilling her parents' expectations for her are the prerequisite for her mission trip to the Dominican Republic. Now she is uncertain about wanting to go away at all. Her attachment with her parents is weak and her resistance to them is strong.

Annie's parents describe her stating that her desire to be good is inside her but they watch in amazement as her good intentions take a flip and her impulses take over.

Annie's parents see her as strong-willed, oppositional, defiant, disobedient, ungrateful, and negative. I see Annie as an untethered child at risk of becoming preoccupied with the family taboos (drugs, not working hard and sex). My sense is that with all the pressure on Annie to be good she will continue to put all of her attachment energy into her peers, resisting both her parents and teachers. Currently, there is no context for parenting Annie.

What's Wrong and What is Needed?

Annie is missing a functional attachment with a responsible adult. Annie is coming undone. She has not experienced an invitation to exist in the presence of a warm, caring adult. Annie needs to experience that she matters, that she is loved, understood and known inside out. She needs to feel the warmth of safety and acceptance for all of her so that she can grow into maturity. Her attachments with her parents need to deepen. Both parents need to give care and grace to the other so that they find

the energy inside themselves to bring Annie to **rest** inside the parental relationship. Inside the parent relationship, Annie need to find her tears so that the dam can break and unleash all the pent up toxicity that has held back nature's master plan from unfolding as it should. She needs to know that she can't get everything that she wants, that life won't always go her way and that she can survive making mistakes and encountering disappointments. Highly sensitive to, and afraid of, becoming a unique person, Annie senses that she is no longer welcome at her parents' table and is seeking a place with her friends. Annie's parents need to see the fragile sense of self that drives Annie into the arms of her unguided and immature peers where she can be easily led into self-destruction.

Treatment/Progress

Between June and September, Annie's parents worked with me for nine sessions, attended two of my seminars ("Understanding the Teenage Brain" and "Counterwill") and introduced me to a couple from their church who provided respite for them over a two month period. Annie's parents had great difficulty letting go of the leverage that consequences, time-outs and the church has provided for them. The developmental model was so antithetical to their teachings that it took a lot of coaching as they worked their way through the maze.

During our fourth session, I was aware that Annie's mother softened and tears streamed down her cheek. She explained that she felt tremendous guilt that she hadn't noticed Annie's alarm. The tears were quiet at first and moved into heavy sobbing. I indicated (with my hand) to her husband to stay quiet. Saying nothing, he moved in when she took a huge breath and held her close. The paradigm silently began to shift into place.

Annie's parents were adamant that they wanted to have safeguards in place before they brought her home. I explained that unfortunately, there are no cognitive tricks that can provide them the structure that they wanted in order for them to feel safe. Putting the responsibility for being good and healing the family on Annie alone would only provoke more feelings of frustration inside of her. I explained that having Annie back home would create feelings of regret, uncertainty, sadness and fear in them and that this is what nature intended in our owning our own feelings. I agreed to work with the mother as her feelings unfolded while grieving all that had not worked in her parenting Annie. The greatest challenge for the mother was to find her desire to take charge of her daughter. It was not her choice to have

Annie live with the family. Her husband wanted Annie because she is his niece and this is the "right thing" to do.

By the fifth session, the husk of the attachment seed was broken and it was starting to sprout. I talked briefly about what my eyes saw and continued with the plant metaphor. I explained that some of the resistance (to step in and take charge) which they felt from time to time was like the soil above any seed. It is hard to push through but the pushing forces us to gather strength for finding the patience to grow slowly with our expectations. The father mused that maybe Annie is like that seed in that she needs to push and resist so that she can gather the strength to live her life in a chaotic world.

The next week I received an email from the mother, who also provides care for the elderly. She had invited Annie to work with her for the rest of the summer! I heard nothing for two weeks after this and I lived with the hope that the bridge between mother and daughter was being reinforced through their caring for others. Rekindling a mother's love may have shed a softer light on Annie's woundedness.

Annie's parents lost their confidence when she took off with a few of her friends. On a Friday afternoon, without asking for permission, she left her job at a fast-food restaurant, called an acquaintance and joined a group of teenagers heading to the beach. It had not occurred to the parents that Annie's frustration was building working in a noisy environment with bells and whistles going off at unpredictable times. Two jobs might have been too much for her to handle. Her only way out of her frustration was to avoid a stand-off with her parents and to run with her peers. Annie's parents took a soft approach when she returned home. I encouraged them to state their values with Annie but to give up on enforcing them. The parents sat together in grief about all that wasn't working.

With the parents' recognition that eruptions can be provoked, my most recent suggestion to them was to search for more delicate interpretations of what they were seeing. They agreed to look for ways to reduce the pressure rather than increasing it.

There have been no signs of foul frustration for a year now. I met with the school counsellor who has become a safe haven for Annie in her school. Her mother continues to come alongside her gently, engaging Annie's attachment energy when she has the opportunity. Her adoptive father has stopped "trying to talk sense into Annie" with his sarcasm, teasing and humour/put-downs. Annie has found meaning and purpose with an older woman in her church for whom she provides care.

Annie's mother reports that Annie too has found her tears and is living a fuller life with a wider perspective. No longer is Annie opposed to having more than one point of view. Her parents are also able to sit with some inner dissonance, wait before they speak, find a time when they can see Annie in a good light and work with her outside some of the incidents.

Alarm has played an important role in the stuckness of this family. Their primitive brains had the upper hand in many of the family's troubling situations. When things slowed down enough for the cortisol and adrenaline levels to drop, the frontal cortex was able to engage and give direction for developmental progress. When the parents found their good intentions, their impulses were trumped and the necessary mixing in the prefrontal cortex could take place. Annie's parents saw her differently, responded differently to her and she to them.

Addendum, 2014

Loyalty Within Boundaries: Being Known and Being Safe

Question:

One of the roots of attachment is to be known. Another root is loyalty and belonging. Does this mean that parents' secrets should be known to their children and parents should share information about the siblings to one another?

Answer:

Loyalty to the family legacy both past and future can preserve a sense of pride. Disloyalty in the family is rarely defined or understood yet is the greatest source of hurt that gets in the way of emotional regulation or feeling emotionally safe inside the womb of relationship. The dynamics of trust, fairness and entitlement are ultimately disturbed and maturation compromised.

The family context has always been promoted as where the experience of relating, giving and receiving begins and a place from which to express honest emotions and thoughts. What has been lost is the sensitivity to the damage that can unfold as the result of unintentional destructive interventions into an intricate system that requires both being known and being kept safe.

Parenting practices which are loyal to ensuring the honour and separateness of each child provide an emotionally supportive environment in which children can mature. Being heard and known is necessary to gain a sense of self before being able to figure out how best to fit into the larger world. A parent's capacity to maintain boundaries among their children is critical in the growth and maturation of each child. It is the parent and eventually the primary partner who is intended to know one inside out not the siblings nor their partners nor FaceBook friends. Exposure of anyone's vulnerabilities hurts.

Vertical relationships are those in which the parent is positioned at the top of the hierarchy where children of all ages can enter without judgment to share their joys, hurts and confusions. Information flow is from bottom-up, never top-down. Parents who share their personal secrets with children (top-down) disturb the ties that bind and the confidence that the child (of any age) has in feeling safe inside the family. Usually this is possible until the parent is fragile or old-old. Horizontal relationships or those among the siblings can be supportive but it is up to the siblings to choose what they want to share; the parent who "knows all" must protect the integrity of each sibling by not taking information from "one house to another".

Parents were never intended to call in the support of their children in order to problem solve within the family. Parenting is all about giving life and then fostering life to individuals who can alone and together cope with life itself. In order to do this, it is a delicate balance between providing a place to be known and cultivating a place to be safe.

Loyalty to Lineage Legacy and the Land

Newfoundland is a time capsule where accents, music, words and practices have continued unabated while they are dying out in the rest of the world. Magnificent, ancient roots of humble beginnings continue to reach to the secrets of the past through traditions of song; storytelling, knitting, rug hooking and folklore, anchoring people to this place both physically and spiritually forever. With over 9600 kilometres of coastline, Newfoundland is inextricably linked to the sea. Families take the responsibility of nourishing the roots that bind people together, recognizing that moral values are finely interlaced into the culture so that it can continue to exist. Donna Morrissey a Newfoundland writer shares through one of her characters, Clair, in a novel that unfolds a story of family life in Newfoundland, "We are the walking roots of our souls and we must nourish what is underneath".

The oral tradition of storytelling, full of reminders of the social and ecological resilience of the Newfoundland people preserves history, creates a community of embeddedness and fosters invisible ties that bind. Running through these stories are qualities of perseverance, innovation, courage and generosity. Having a sense of place and a sense of belonging to the past gives a source of attachment pride which keeps people motivated to work hard, trusting that if help is needed it is as close as one's neighbour.

Folklore, story and song provide the vehicles for inculcating moral values in each generation. Driven by empathy, or by a sense of fairness or simply by gut reactions, the code for living a life under adverse conditions has cultivated an adaptable, resilient people who graciously reach out with an invitation for others to exist in their space. Woven from strong connections to the land and the sea, the threads running throughout Newfoundland are both strong and resilient.

Loyalty to the family legacy both past and future has preserved a sense of pride. One young woman, in her early 20's, with whom I spoke exclaimed, "Why would I want to ever leave this place? I have everything I need; the sea, the land and my family". Indeed, there is something about the size of the province which allows people to meet and to know each other and to celebrate the past, the present and the promise of the future. Influenced by a rich cross-disciplined culture, people who leave keep coming back to fill-up with the unburdened gentleness of their relationships to the land, their legacy and their lineage.

To know that two of my grandchildren will be raised as Newfoundlanders, on this island, self-contained and out of the mainstream, gives me joy. My son explained that multigenerational events are common. "Newfoundlanders hold on to their kids longer and being together (grandparents, parents and children) is important". If we want what we want in our lives for the people who made us, my yearning for a life that is about the people you love, is now being manifested in the life my children (Deb and Jason) chose in being Newfoundlanders. For me, I can now put down a grandmother root in their province and feel real.

-0-

Regret and Resilience: Aging Well

As the New Year approaches and I realize that I am now referred to as a Senior Citizen, I see the future diminishing and recognize that this is a time to reconcile my multitude of regrets. It feels like an existential wake-up call where I want to undo the digital culture, unfriend people who didn't take me seriously, unfollow some of the directions which I have taken in life that led me to things that I want to change but cannot. I regret that I wasn't a more loving daughter, a more present parent and now a more compassionate wife. It seems to me that to strive to live a life without regret is impossible. Taking this position helps me to consider that regret

may not be as negative an experience as I thought until today. Perhaps it has been the lens through which I have viewed my regrets that have made them cringe worthy.

Regret really says something about what one's life's goals are all about. Regret doesn't have to remind us of what we did badly but can remind us that we know we can do better. Helen Keller told us that character cannot be developed in ease and quiet. It is only through experiences of trial, loss and suffering that our vision can be cleared, ambition inspired and success achieved. Living and finishing well is an exercise of integrating regret, loss and grief into building the character of an individual. There is a growing body of research showing that people who have psychological capital have a sense of well-being across the lifespan.

We tend to be familiar with intellectual capital, which is what people know; and social capital, which is who they know. Psychological capital is who you are and is made up of four virtues:

confidence, hope, optimism and resilience. Resilience is a process of adaptation, which cultivates hope, confidence and optimism. The adaptive process refers to that natural growth life force by which we are changed, where we develop emotionally or learn a new reality as a result of coming to terms with something that cannot be changed. This is a process by which we learn from our mistakes and benefit from failure. This is also the process by which adversity changes our character for the better.

Regret is a frontal cortex activity and to regret is an indication that we are fully functional, human and humane. Tears are nature's way of providing the brain with the mechanism to adapt to the futility of regret. In that place of futility, of not being able to change the past, to undo the mistake or to replace the loss, there is nothing left to do but cry. Tears are part of nature's plan in helping us to integrate life's regrets.

Tears of regret are existential and unavoidable and part of the recalibration of the brain's

resilience. Living, aging, and finishing well is all about having successful internalizations or integration of regret into the maze of a life well lived.

In cultivating a personal context for aging well, a story is essential in first making sense of failure, living with what can't be changed, seeing that we can survive adversity and coming to a point of realization. Having that realization throws us into the richness of being in the present moment. In that richness, there are infinite possibilities in what is left to enjoy as opposed to sinking into a cultural Kool-Aid where lamenting things that occurred in the past – what is done is done according to Lady Macbeth.

-0-

Homesick, Hungry, Tired and Bored

Question:

My daughter often makes these very four different statements that I suspect originate from very different attachment-based needs. Could you please help me to better understand how to handle each sign of emptiness in a sensitive manner.

Answer:

You are absolutely correct. All four emotional states are indicators that something is missing.

1) *"I want to go home".* When this statement is made and your daughter is physically in her own home, it might indicate a moment of emotional discomfort. Being at "home" is like being at rest inside a safe emotional relationship where there is no need to pursue closeness. Rather than respond with: "But you are at home!"; you could open your inviting arms stating: "Come here, I know what you need right now". A look in your eyes of love and a big hug generated from your warm heart and with as few words as possible will lower the sense of being lost and bring her into a state of emotional regulation. When she feels safe in the safety of your presence, it is likely that she will disclose the antecedent to feeling lost.

2) *"I'm hungry (while eating or as soon as she sees me)".* Hunger is also an emotional indicator of starving for connection inside of relationship. Relationships well rooted in feeling a sense of sameness, belonging, loyalty, significance (mattering), loved and being understood will satiate a yearning to feel full. You might want to review your daughter's relationship pursuits. If she has been connecting on-

line through texting or FaceBook, she may well be frustrated and hungry for an emotionally meaningful relationship. The current simplification and reduction of relationship to on-line connections spoil the appetite for what children really need. When healthy adult relationships are displaced for a plethora of reasons, hunger results. Your best bet is to tell your daughter that you know what she needs and get involved with all your senses present and be interested in her interests.

3) *"I'm tired"*. Emotional tiredness because of too much worry, too much stimulation, too much thinking, too much pursuit of emotional closeness and feeling the depth of sorrow or passion could be approached by inviting your daughter to lie on the ground beside you to watch the clouds or watch the grasses blow. Perhaps a walk through a natural

setting which will stimulate her senses will reboot her brain so that she can feel refreshed. Access to solitude is a good antidote to any child's tired life.

4) *"I'm bored"*. Childhood boredom has apparently been outlawed by today's adults and we continue to add layers of entertainment (including the introduction of iPotty in 2013 to ensure entertaining poops) which creates an atmosphere of manic disruption and leaves children in a state of continuous partial attention. What is the cost of fearing boredom? What worthy things might we have thoughtlessly left behind? Solitude now causes discomfort but that discomfort is often the stimulus to a healthy and inspiring activity. Encouraging daydreaming will help your daughter to get in touch with her gift of creativity. You could suggest that she sit on the

porch or lie on her bed staring out the window until her good mind gives her an idea. Just as we decide to limit our intake of sugars and fats, we must decide to limit entertainment and "over-the-top" experiences for our children.

Below the surface of each of the above four statements is the **same** unmet need. Hearing the theme of her statement and responding with a warm invitation for her to exist in your presence, whatever her emotional state, is an opportunity to spark the engine of development. Giving her the quiet space, meeting her relationship needs is often all that is required to find the solutions for fulfilling her basic emotional needs. She will then move on: secure, satiated, rested and motivated to take the steering wheel of her life. Reclaiming what we've lost in letting ourselves feel an absence of stimulation will ultimately give us a space to cultivate what we really need and that is a full

relationship meal not the teaser of offering a cookie.

-0-

Anxious Parents – Anxious Kids: Getting off the Anxiety-Go-Round

The brain develops habits, including habits of responding to feelings of not being safe. When the alarm system in the brain registers unsafe conditions, it doesn't have a lot of range in prioritizing the risk of danger. Fully operational at birth, the amygdala or smoke alarm in the centre of the brain is hypervigilant in its efforts to bring us to caution. The more sensitive it is to the environment, the more repetitive the response translates into anxiety.

Most often, parents and children try to manage anxiety by avoiding the stimulus. Unintentionally, fears are ramped up by constructing an anxiety-avoiding system. The problem with avoidance is that it works and often isolation from the "real" world occurs. It is not what we are worried about that is the problem but the way our bodies and minds react.

Human brains are evolved to adapt to the environment in which they are placed. If the way we think about anxiety moves us to develop strategies to avoid it, we are missing the opportunity to cope with life itself.

Most kids and adults with anxiety are highly energized. Ruminating about a worry makes a worry rut in the brain, worries are created and guaranteed to draw the worrier into the rabbit hole. Why not use that high drive and energy to block going down the worry path; using persistence to go down a different path. Thought stopping was first introduced by Psychologist, David Burns before the neuroscience of anxiety was understood. Now managing anxiety involves not only stopping the thought but replacing the thought with something else that has a more positive impact. In her July, 2014 on-line "Psychotherapy Networker" course, Lynn Lyons suggests that parents can help kids to expect anxiety will happen, encourage them to externalize it

and then experiment how to get out of it.

Remember, the amygdala has two parts. The right side of the amygdala learns fear and the left side asks questions like: "Is this a place to be fearful?. After the logical left side reviews the potential for danger, it can say to the right side: "It's okay, this isn't really scary". The fear has permission to shrink away. Be prepared to slow down, take small steps and remember it is all about plunging into anxiety, assessing the rationality behind it and then living through it. Talking to kids about their world, finding ways to handle life's twists and turns not protecting them from life itself fosters maturation. The transformative power that comes from regulating emotions grows from a state of feeling emotionally safe. This is the essence of development.

-0-

Coaching: an Alternative to Psychotherapy

Question:

I'm really dissatisfied with the way my life is going at the moment. My work, my family and my relationships seem to be less than I want. I don't think I need therapy but I'm not sure what would be helpful. What do you suggest?

Answer:

What you might consider is getting some coaching as opposed to psychotherapy or counselling. Many of my individual clients and those who attend my courses and seminars are actually being coached as opposed to engaging in therapy.

Coaches and psychotherapists use similar skills: being aware of, understanding and appreciating feelings; looking at all sides of problems, and helping their clients to achieve their full potential. There are also coaches who help their clients to focus on a single problem or set of related problems.

Traditionally, psychotherapy has had its roots in psychopathology or some form of clinical problem and many would say that it's part of the illness-model of health care. Coaching, on the other hand, focuses on human strengths, positive personal goals and untapped possibilities. Rather than serve as a *healer*, the coach acts as a *facilitator* who guides clients through emotional fault lines and into new territory. There are some therapists who are "*solution focused*" as opposed to being oriented to the client's *problems*. They help to articulate the client's current resources and possible solutions rather than concentrate on the origins of the problem. Coaches take somewhat the same approach and work with their clients to give them immediate feedback and encouragement as new directions and behviours are explored.

Individuals who want to make changes in how they interact with both family members and friends may want to begin by calling a relationship coach – someone who can broaden their perspective on how individuals operate as part of larger systems. Or, sometimes, the focus in on understanding the developmental stage of the client's children and what each child can and cannot understand. This can make a huge difference in the way we communicate and the type of relationship we establish with our children.

A coach can help to define beliefs and can offer encouragement to focus on personal authenticity, creating realistic roadmaps for achieving more depth, meaning and clarity in interaction with others.

And one of the benefits of coaching is that sessions can be held through interactive media such as Skype or Facetime. While some therapists also use these, that is far less common because of concerns about privacy and because non-verbal and vocal cues are frequently lost when the interaction takes place on small screens.

-0-

When the Look of Love is Missing: Emotional Dysregulation Occurs

No matter what our age, we are all questing for safety in relationships. Our bodies have a need to engage and to bond with others. In fact, the feeling of being connected to another is a biological imperative which gives us the capacity to emotionally and physiologically regulate or dysregulate one another. The regulators of body chemistry and emotional well-being are found in our relationships. Trauma breaks down this feeling of connectedness and safety and interferes with healthy co-regulation, and thus, mental health issues arise.

The negotiation of safety is the preamble to forming *attachments*. The cues are subtle and appear in the upper part of the face first. Our "crow's feet" (the wrinkles around our eyes) are powerful cues to excitement, feeling and connectedness. We naturally look at the eyes of others and unconsciously evaluate the features of a smile. A baby searches out our gaze and focuses on our eyes to be able to interpret our behaviour.

Specific neural pathways exist to promote the experience of feeling safe – a feeling which is understood at a bodily or visceral level. These pathways manage the muscles of the face, control our gaze, create facial expression and head gestures and give us the ability to listen. The intonation and rhythm of our voices, as well as our posture while engaging with others reflect our inner state to the other. These processes are the variables for cultivating and growing safe emotional relationships where we can be ourselves and fit into the larger community.

The nervous system detects risk factors in others without our awareness. If danger is sensed (likely by the amygdala), the body's defenses are mobilized; the chemistry of alarm is generated; safety is compromised, and the conditions for the establishment of trusting relationships are shut down – perhaps permanently if the alarm is prolonged and serious.

A child who sees a parent's face go flat or expressionless moves into a state of fear and experiences the loneliness of *detachment*. An adult, who gazes into the eyes of another looking for the warmth of invitation and can't find it, feels uncomfortable, frustrated and rejected. A child who is shunned by a teacher becomes difficult to manage behaviourally. An adult who is repeatedly provoked by a partner's eye-rolling or look of disapproval will be at high risk of sinking into a state of anxious relating or depression.

Our behaviour is based on a physiological response to feeling safe. We are wired to hear the tone of soft melodic voices and to see an accepting expression on others' faces. Our body and our emotional system can detect danger and disturbance in another. Any tone of voice that is above or below the range that the middle ear can comfortably tolerate will provoke anxiety. Connectedness is dependent upon situations where there is no anxiety; situations in which we feel safe. When the look of love is missing, in any important relationship, emotional dys-regulation results. It may be wise to think about the impact of our relationships on the mental health and brain development of the people who are important to us or who depend on us for their growth.

-0-

Index

A

abandon, 154
abandoned, 127, 146, 148
abandonment, 153
abbess, 139
abelard, 139
abilities, 80, 103
ability, 10, 12-13, 21-22, 24, 44-45, 72, 75, 80, 89, 102, 112, 117-118, 130-131, 172
absence, 13, 168
absenteeism, 151
abuse, 24, 42
abused, 108-109
academic, 29, 88, 117, 121-122, 124
academics, 87
acceptance, 5, 24-25, 28, 62, 87, 93, 105, 119, 156
accepted, 29, 87, 92, 109, 122, 135
accepting, 27, 72, 89, 94, 172
accusations, 9, 78
accused, 9
achieved, 87, 138, 164
achievement, 29, 80
achievements, 91, 137
achieving, 171
acknowledgment, 119
action, 5, 41, 75, 88, 98, 105, 107, 123
actions, 13, 65, 69, 93, 127
activate, 41, 82
activated, 27, 40-41
activates, 110
adapt, 42, 44, 53, 78, 89, 91, 165, 169

adaptability, 31
adaptable, 163
adaptation, 36, 44, 64, 76, 165
adapted, 80, 112, 147
adapting, 46, 147
adaptive, 37, 75-76, 127, 142, 147, 149, 151, 165
ADHD, 80
adolescence, 15, 43, 77
adolescent, 8, 39, 86, 98, 135
adolescents, 7-8, 43, 106, 135
adoption, 28, 93
adoptive, 27, 144-155, 158
adrenal, 82
adrenalin, 28, 152
adrenaline, 11-12, 19, 54, 158
adults, 14-15, 20, 27, 29, 32-33, 39, 43-46, 49, 52, 71, 73, 76-78, 82, 86, 96, 109, 113, 120, 122, 125-126, 129, 131, 134-135, 137, 146-147, 152, 167, 169
advice, 8, 33, 51, 53, 77, 113, 118
affirming, 91
afraid, 20, 46, 53, 93, 112, 145, 147-156
ages, 13, 15, 37, 44-45, 98, 131, 138, 161
aggression, 16, 76, 144, 151
aggressive, 16, 19, 22, 76, 89, 144
aging, 160, 164-165
agitated, 28, 152
alarm, 12, 27-29, 37-39, 49, 56, 58, 60, 69, 76, 78, 82, 89, 110, 125, 127, 130, 141-142, 146-147, 152-153, 157-158, 168, 172
alarmed, 19, 27, 67
alarming, 11-12, 16, 28, 77, 108
alcohol, 42, 106, 144
alibis, 33, 113

B

Index

Index

entertain, 40, 167-168

entitlement, 161

environments, 20, 29, 67, 80, 126

epinephrine, 82

erupt, 108, 125, 127, 144, 146, 158

essence, 36, 77, 91, 98, 137, 169

esteem, 33, 102-103, 108, 113

estrangement, 139

ethics, 139

evolution, 18, 87, 93, 127, 135, 137, 169

excited, 11, 32, 53, 102, 131, 134, 141, 171

existential, 164-165

expectation, 9, 34, 39, 43, 46, 73, 77-78, 87, 93, 98, 109, 114, 124, 127, 137, 147-148, 155, 157

experiences, 8-9, 12, 19, 22-23, 27, 31, 35-38, 42, 44, 59, 65, 72, 75, 77, 82, 87-88, 91, 102-103, 110, 117, 127, 134, 145, 147-149, 152-153, 156, 164, 168, 172

expert, 33, 85, 98-99, 112-113

expressing, 58, 69, 75, 77, 82, 103, 105, 123, 146, 172

eyes, 9, 16, 24, 27, 29, 33, 35, 56, 58, 63, 69, 93, 98, 105, 108, 114, 123, 131, 138, 146, 151, 155, 157, 166, 171-172

F

facebook, 9, 20, 42, 85-86, 161, 167

facetime, 85, 171

facial, 82, 85, 172

failure, 8, 44, 72, 76, 165

fairness, 118, 161, 163

faith, 65, 117, 119

families, 24, 65, 86, 100, 153, 162

feared, 19, 22, 24, 30, 66, 128, 134, 149, 152, 167-169

feeding, 73-74, 100

feeling, 12-13, 17-20, 24, 28-31, 37-38, 40, 42-44, 46, 51, 53, 56, 58, 69, 75-76, 78, 82, 84, 91, 93, 105, 109-110, 119, 130, 134-135, 137, 141, 147, 149-150, 152, 157, 161-162, 166-172

feels, 5, 21, 35, 42, 46, 53, 69, 73, 98, 100, 129, 132-134, 152, 154-155, 164, 166, 172

ferber, 51

financial, 15, 107, 112, 122

finger, 29, 58, 88, 131, 147, 152

fireplace, 29, 56

flow, 46, 54, 56, 87, 116, 141, 162

fmris, 116

focus, 30, 41, 53, 63, 79-80, 83, 99, 103, 116-118, 127, 170-172

folklore, 162-163

forgive, 92-93

forming, 134, 145, 148-155, 171

fostering, 88, 92, 162

fosters, 132, 163, 169

fragile, 9, 60, 69, 82, 108-109, 156, 162

freedom, 15, 65, 96, 118

friendly, 8, 11, 33, 43-44, 85-86, 101, 106, 113, 129, 134, 141-143, 153, 156-157, 161, 170

frustrates, 13, 52-53, 69, 76, 86-89, 91, 93, 107-108, 125, 127, 139, 142, 144, 146-147, 151, 153, 157-158, 167, 172

fulfilled, 35, 42, 86, 91, 98, 135, 138, 153, 155, 168

fundamental, 37, 144, 146

futility, 8, 36, 44, 59-60, 76, 87, 91, 93, 107, 123, 139, 151, 165

G

gabor, 51

generation, 15, 20, 27, 33, 61-62, 91-92, 98, 104, 110, 113, 163

H

I

Index

J

K

L

M

N

Index

presents, 54, 65
pressured, 29, 40, 46, 155
pressures, 82, 112
pride, 127, 161, 163
primary, 49, 52, 58, 94, 103, 118, 161
principal, 12, 89, 124
privileges, 12, 29, 124
problems, 16, 32, 37, 43, 46, 51, 67, 71, 76, 80, 82, 98, 116, 134, 155, 170
processes, 16, 102, 110, 116, 118, 172
procrastination, 39
profanity, 127, 142
professional, 71, 82, 90, 104, 126, 139
programs, 20, 98, 101, 112, 118
proposal, 63, 92, 106, 122
protected, 23, 32, 37, 39, 46, 85, 146, 169
providers, 33, 40, 88, 95-96, 113, 120, 135
provides, 37, 60, 63, 116, 134, 157-158
provoke, 12, 22, 147, 157-158, 172
proximity, 37, 49, 118, 147
psychological, 16, 30, 52, 100, 118, 153, 155, 164
psychologist, 22, 75, 80, 88-89, 96, 107, 137, 169
psychology, 19, 21, 37, 96, 119, 131, 134
psychopathology, 43, 170
psychotherapy, 5, 104, 106-107, 110, 136, 160, 169-170
puberty, 44
pubic, 141
pupils, 131, 145
pursuit, 85, 93, 118, 141, 147, 166-167

Q

quest, 6, 22, 35, 117, 119, 137-138, 171
questions, 54, 58, 119, 169

R

rage, 54, 82
rape, 19
react, 12, 19, 22, 40, 51, 75, 85, 110, 163, 169
reactive, 24
reacts, 155
reality, 75, 93, 165
reassurance, 12, 27, 58, 77, 102, 119, 125, 131, 135
recalibration, 165
recess, 124
recession, 5, 91, 112
recipe, 5, 96, 102
refugee, 19-20
refuse, 69, 73, 107, 127, 142, 146, 150, 155
regulate, 48-49, 52, 64, 75-77, 82, 102-103, 110-111, 129, 136, 161, 166, 169, 171
rehabilitation, 35, 60
rejection, 23, 37, 69, 73, 127, 134, 137, 172
relationships, 5, 10, 12-14, 20, 24, 27, 30, 33-34, 37, 40, 44, 46-47, 49, 52, 57, 63, 73, 78-79, 82-83, 85-88, 93, 95-100, 102-103, 105, 107-108, 113-114, 116-118, 124, 126-128, 134-139, 141-142, 144-146, 148-156, 161-163, 166-168, 170-173
relax, 59, 125, 127, 137
religious, 15, 65, 147
resilience, 32, 38, 44, 49, 76, 79, 87,

Index

T

U

V

39845067R00107

Made in the USA
Charleston, SC
19 March 2015